Acknowledgements

I am indebted to all the people and patients w
humbled to share with, in their most vulnerat

I have looked back on all my experiences from
different from how others remember the time

I have changed some peoples names to protect their identity. I may have
inadvertently mixed up time sequences but have tried to remember as best I
could. I have tried to be honest and fair in my recollection of people, places and
times so apologies if I have made any errors.

I have been in awe of many colleagues who have taught me so much by example
as they sought to alleviate the suffering of their patients.

Thankyou to Rosie Jamieson for critiquing my rough work and giving me
structure to work to.

To all those who encouraged me in my writing, thankyou for your faith in me and
kind comments.

To my amazing family who put up with my twittering and ideas for my book,
thankyou. You are my greatest achievement and I am proud of each of you, Hazel,
Rosalind and Blair. To my beautiful grandchildren who bring me great joy,
thankyou Jessica, Ailsa, Rory and Phoebe.

Thankyou to my husband who is a constant source of support and love.

To Gemma a dear friend + colleague

from

P

Prologue

The book is a humorous and poignant reflection of a trainee nurse and midwifery student in the 1970s in Scotland. It is partly autobiographical and mostly an anecdotal recount of the incredible people the author encountered in a varied and extremely interesting 40 year nursing career. You will meet some fascinating characters, some who will make you laugh, others will make you cry and occasionally some you will despise.

This was a time of great change in the NHS as it was moving from the paternalistic cottage hospitals model of care, to a more centralised beaurocracy. It was a time when there were very many characters who were the norm in the 1970's in nursing and midwifery.

Lorna is third eldest in a family of 8 children whose father was a complex character, he could be nice then melancholic and was sometimes a violent alcoholic.

Come on a journey with Lorna as she encounters the most fascinating people that she worked with and the patients whose lives she touched. Many of these patients more importantly impacted her life in many ways

Chapter One

Where it all began;

Laugh? I nearly cried with joy at such kindness from a lady who I have held in the deepest regard since the first day I met her.

Miss Rodgers was an exemplary matron, she was a diminutive lady, just shy of 5 feet in height, with a shock of white hair and upright posture. She spoke quietly and kindly and was very much a hands on matron.

We all loved having this lovely lady who seemed ancient to me, a teenager at the time. She would probably been in her late 50's in 1975, but as a teenager anyone over 30 was just about past their prime in my eyes.

Miss Rodger had lived through the second world war and rumour had it that she never married following the death of her sweetheart in the war.

I hope you don't mind but I have made up your off duty and have given you all early shifts in the meantime, as I do not like to think of you walking along that road to the bus in the dark.

 Well I have to say I did not mind at all and as a naive sixteen year old, I did not at first realise how kind this older matron was being to me and that indeed she was one of a dying breed of nurses who were wed to the job.

I was the third oldest in a some what dysfunctional family of ten and at that point in my life in the late 1970's I was just looking for a career. So lacking imagination I went into nursing as my mother and older sister had done so before me.

It was funny really because when I look back to that period in my life the only discussions I had about career were with the careers officer who came to the school in our third year. After asking me what I wanted to do, she advised me that I should get an application in for a job at a factory which was being built in the town.

When I say discussion she asked in a brusque manner, well what do you want to do for work? I replied I wasn't quite sure and had been considering joinery or possibly nursing. I obviously took to long in my considerations or just looked like a no hoper who was wasting her valuable time. Which is why she brushed me off with the advice re the "factory". She obviously hadn't even checked what type of factory it was, as it turned out to be a petro chemical plant and no hopers would not have been suitable. I did indeed in later years work at the plant as an Occupational Health Nurse.

Although I was not sure of what I wanted to do I did realise that I most certainly did not want to do factory work which to my mind was a drudge. Don't get me wrong, I am not denigrating factory work it was just not something I enjoyed, it would not do if we all wanted to do the same thing.

Albeit my first job before nursing was in a clothing factory where I stayed for 9 months before starting as an auxillary. I was a dreadful machinist and when I look back I was amazed they didn't sack me. I even made mistakes sewing the iconic jockey motifs on mens Y fronts with an automatic machine. I was quite bored and my mind wandered and so did the machine. I just could not understand how the women I worked beside could stand the place and work. Their heads were down all the time as they chatted away and got through a considerable bundle of garments. I would ask them how many years they had worked in the factory and the average was 12 years! Oh my word how could they stand it?

The machinists loved the extra money they made for going above their tally. As for me, I used to escape a lot and go and sit in the toilets composing and writing poems. My supervisor Mary would remark, what a weak bladder you have Lorna.

I did discover when working in the factory that the men were paid almost double what I was paid and this didn't sit right with me. I enquired of the supervisor why this was as they were doing the same and sometimes less skilled work than us machinists. Her response was typical of the reason why it took so long to get anywhere near equal pay. She replied its because he is a man Lorna and he has to provide for his family. I was astounded that these women found this acceptable to be paid half of what a man earns. This was 1976 and it was 6 years since the introduction of the equal pay act and it does take time to change mindset. However even fifty years later there is still disparity between what men and women are paid. Its not right and its not fair.

I did think it would be nice to be an electrician or joiner but in the 1970's it was nigh impossible for anyone to take me seriously and offer a female an apprenticeship. Once again I believed it was evidence of a patriachal society which favours the males in most areas of life.

I remember vague discussions regarding entering nursing with my mother who had been a dux medallist at school but was constrained by her family to work. In the late 1940's working class people did not go to college or university as they could not afford to send their children. They depended on the income their job, however small the contribution would bring. So right from awareness as a child, mother knew that dreams and aspirations were for others and she had to conform to family and generational expectations.

Her teacher Mr Terris a lovely bachelor and very fine gentleman went to mums house to plead with her family to give her the opportunity to go to university but it fell on deaf ears as money was tight.

Mr Terris was a visionary and an exemplary teacher for his time. I had the pleasure of being one of his students in languages in his final year of teaching. He was a lovely man. I recall being in his class and in his quiet and dignified manner he was making his way around all his pupils to assist them. As he bent over to point out something to one of my classmates, two of the unruly boys spat on the back of his tweed blazer. It was heart breaking to see him being made such a fool of and for these boys to show such disrespect to this fine man. I would have hated to witness the embarrassment he would have felt on discovering this disgusting mess. He deserved so much more from those wee toerags he was trying to help.

Mother then went and got a job in Banks fruit and flower shop, which is where she met my dad and a romance blossomed. She had a tough life with my father who was a complex character, who became a violent alcoholic and would often beat her and us. He wasn't all bad but as a child our home atmosphere was oppressive and we often lived in fear.

As an adult I can look back and can analyse dad to a degree but as a child it was difficult. I loved him but often did not like him very much. Yet his other drinking pals saw him as the life and soul of the party. Dad could be nice but he had a mercurial temperament and his temper was triggered by the smallest of things and was volcanic in nature. As a nurse and adult I was able to attribute this to many aspects of his life which I will describe later.

When my mother was 40 yrs of age and having had her 8 children she went to do her nurse training but could only do enrollment nursing. This was because registered nursing training involved travelling to different parts of Fife and being resident at times and my father would not countenance this.

I recall when she had finished her training and was looking for a job as an enrolled nurse she was unable to get beyond the application stage. When she eventually stopped admitting on the application forms that she had 8 children, she got the next job she applied for.

Our dad was a difficult man and did not like mum working or going to college, she had a tough life with him as did we. He did however like the money that her wage contributed to the household income as you can imagine the outlay for a house of 10 people.

So the fact that she even managed to do her training and apply herself to make time for studying makes me both proud of her and sad that she was held back throughout her life to fulfil her potential.

Enrolled Nurse training was traditionally done with a shorter course of 18 months duration. They were a division two nurse who would work under the supervision of a registered nurse, and carry out various tasks assigned to them.

It suited many young mums or those who felt they were not academic enough to undertake a 3 year course at college and have greater responsibility once qualified. An Enrolled Nurse was looked on as a more personal nurse as they were more hands on since they didn't have ward management responsibility.

I met a great deal of excellent enrolled nurses in my long career who were much more knowledgeable than me. There are still Enrolled nurses employed to this day in Australia but in the UK single registration in 1980s mostly forced the phasing out of Enrolled nurses.

Mother advised me to go for general registration as that would give me a career and not be stuck in a rut as she felt she was.

However at this stage and being only 16 I had to find a job prior being accepted for nurse training at the age of 17 and following a successful interview I started my nursing career at the Northern General Hospital in Dunfermline as an auxillary nurse.

Although the Northern had started life as a Victorian workhouse and eerily enough was situated right beside the graveyard, it was a nice place to work.

I always thought that admission to the workhouse must have felt like the end of the line for inmates of the workhouse. No safety net of a welfare state at that time in history and then you are reduced to the dregs of society. That is until the day the ground claimed you next door in the cemetary, what a depressing view and such a sad life.

The hospital had gone through many changes as a fever hospital and many other things, and was currently being used as a three bed ward for geriatrics or the elderly as we refer to them now. I was assigned to ward three a sixteen bed ward with sister Kolber in charge. I was sixteen and very much the baby of the hospital and very soon became adopted bairn by the older nurses who taught me a great deal. Sister Kolber took me under her wing and taught me a lot of the basics of nursing. She also invited me back to her home for meals and even took me on holiday with her husband in their caravan. It was very kind of her and I enjoyed her company, although when she advised me to take elocution lessons to eradicate my accent, I was surprised. She did it with the best of intentions as she felt my accent might hold me back in life and in some ways I understood how people unfairly judge a person. I never did go for elocution lessons and so far I have been understood by all my patients and have achieved a great deal in my career despite the prejudicial views of a minority.

I have endured more at the hands of bullies who exist in every walk of life and the nepotisim that causes such unrest in a workplace. I have risen above such folk as my faith sustains me and I feel sorry for folk who behave in this negative manner as it must affect their mental health ultimately.

One of my favourite nurses was Lucy a lady in her late fifties who was a senior enrolled nurse who had been an auxiliary nurse like me but had gained promotion in house during the early post war years. Lucy was a petite bundle of fun who just loved the elderly and loved to have fun with them. She always wore stockings and suspenders not for titillation but that was what she was used to, which amused me no end but more so the elderly men. One day when we were bed bathing an old gent, Lucy winked at me and then lifted the hem of her dress to show off said suspenders to the old man, making sure she had caught his eye first and he just chuckled and chuckled. I was red with embarrassment but realised it was innocent fun.

I of course had many firsts at the hospital, witnessing my first death which seemed quite surreal and especially given the casual way the nurse told me that I should go and see Jeannie as she had just died. I was incredulous and exclaimed you're messing but no I was assured she was dead so go along and see. The nurse came with me and as I looked at a calm and serene Jeannie with her long grey pigtails I again said she is not dead she's sleeping, well put your head beside hers and feel for her breath on your cheek. I felt none but was still unconvinced as at this point she let out expired air, see I said. The nurse was bemused at my incredulity and doubt and told me to get a metal spoon and put it underneath her nostrils and if it became moist she was breathing and if not then indeed she was dead.

Of course she was dead and I finally realised but I could not understand how someone I was talking with just a wee while earlier, just died, it was a real shock to me.

However I was privileged to witness great care and dignity with which the nurses took when preparing last offices with Jeannie.

That was when nurses wash and prepare the body for the relatives to see prior to be taken away by the undertaker. All throughout the last offices the nurse spoke with kindness and compassion to a lady whose lifeblood was stilled and last breath was gone as if she could hear.

I felt I was a privileged observer at a humbling experience and that has lasted with me all my career as I have looked after many dead patients through last offices.

I recall going back to the ward and getting on with the routines of dressing and washing patients and tending to their needs. Miss Rodger was passing and stopped me to ask if I would mind giving her a wee hand. She explained Mr Smith had been doubly incontinent and needed cleaning and his bed changed. Of course I didn't mind and said I would do it and take on the less favourable job of cleaning Mr Smith. This lovely lady insisted that no she would do that part if I just position and hold the bedbound Mr Smith, as she didn't want me to be put off a nursing career. She was a wee gem and I have only on a few occasions worked with managers who led by example, and were willing to be hands on when required.

Once I became comfortable in the routine of a hospital ward I started to relax and joke with my colleagues and played pranks on them such as putting a floors up do not enter notice on the staff changing room. This was only noticed when the matron sent word to find out why the backshift were not yet on duty. The misdemeanour was traced back to me and a wee slap on the wrist later the backshift came on duty.

The matron who was the successor of Miss Rodger was not universally liked as her style of management was completely different. She was to put in the words of one of the staff a nippy wee sweetie. On nightshift she would sneak into the hospital and take off her shoes to avoid being heard in an effort to catch the staff out at whatever misdemeaner she hoped to find. Indeed she must have been cock-a-hoop when on one night she found a nurse sleeping, I'm not sure of all the details but the nurse who was due to retire that year had indeed closed her eyes and was caught by the matron. She was sacked and struck off the nursing register and I believe lost her pension.

It was a lovely place to work and filled with many characters such as Jane the older auxiliary who made a great show of taking her false teeth out to eat and Grace another enrolled nurse who befitted her name wonderfully as she was grace personified. Many years later I met her after she had had a double mastectomy for breast cancer but was surviving well.

The patients were also a hoot and I still recall many of them, Tibby a frail old lady with a multitude of coloured bed socks who was quite pernickety and demanding. I suppose when you have nothing to do all day you probably start navel gazing as it were and potentially every twinge becomes an issue and demands attention.

The institutionalisation of the elderly in the 1970s was well meaning and paternalistic, but denied many older people a normal and full life. We medicalised the normal process of aging and reduced the range of life experiences to the elderly, albeit with good intent.

Rose an Aberdonian who at 96 danced me off my feet at the Scottish dancing, only stopped to tell me her thingy had fallen out again and would I sort it before we got back up tae dance (she had a full rectal prolapse which was sorted by applying a cold pack , astounding)

What a lady she was I loved her to bits and envied her abundant zest for life and energy at such an age.

I loved working with the elderly as they were interesting and such fun but it was always sad to see them dimish physically and mentally due to dementia. I wrote the poem The Long Goodbye around this time as I noticed the interactions of family with their loved mother or father or relative;

The Long Goodbye

Its hard to imagine how it will happen, but
Nestling in the dark recesses of your mind
You consider their death will be swift, with a sense of pathos
And tingled with inevitability. You realise that
Though their influence is great and the time always
Short, there will come a moment when you hope you will
Say a swift goodbye as you let go to new beginnings

You do hope that they will be there long enough to
See you married and enjoy your children and revel
In the joys, tears and successes of your life, but
This long goodbye is most certainly not in your plans
The deterioration and loss of sense and time and reason,
When sense becomes senseless and you recoil at the
Implications of the disease, as it breaks into reality, it hurts

It was an insidious onset with innocuous jokes about

Your terrible memory, worsening with time, then
The denial and cover ups as the shame of truth, that
Nothing would be the same again emerged. Though the
Trauma of watching your faculties diminish along with
Observing the terror etched on your face within lucid moments
Was almost too hard to bear, but for you we endure

So we settle down to contemplate the journey ahead
As we realise it will be a long goodbye. We will consider
How we should prepare for the unknown and how best
To deal with each phase, when all the while we shudder inside
It would have been so much better for you, we think
Or maybe for us had it been swift, leaving us to grieve and then
Cherish memories past of a strong resolute you, forgive us
Then as we stumble through this uncertain and long goodbye

Lorna Finlay (1959-)

The Northern was certainly a good grounding for me on my path to start my student nurse training but first I had to pass the interview process and be offered a place on the course. My application was sent off and the reply letter eagerly anticipated and then the butterflies building as the day for interview approached.

When I informed my colleagues at the hospital that I had an interview they went out of their way to be of help to me and show me and teach me all they could impart before I left for interview. My head was spinning with all the new language of nursing and medicine.

I went to the old cottage hospital for the interview, this was being used as an orthopaedic outpatient and elderly ward at the time. It was one of only two hospitals in Scotland with circular wards. It was demolished a few years later and its signage stone "I was sick and ye visited me" taken to the newer Kirkcaldy hospital.

I was very nervous about making a fool of myself at interview and felt my heat beat faster and my tongue cleave to the roof of my mouth when my name was called for interview by a plump middle aged lady. Miss Junor invited me into the room and in my nervous haste I did not notice the slightly raised room divider and tripped awkwardly into the room. The two interviewers were very kind and politely ignored my entrance and went out of their way to make me feel at ease.

My tongue was still stuck to the roof of my mouth and my pronunciation was awkward as my mind went blank to the first aid question. At this point I felt like leaving the room and going home. However Miss Junor prompted me and at long last in almost a shout as my tongue gained mobility with some long awaited lubrication I forced the correct answer out.

At long last I was offered a place at college but was advised to do the shorter enrolled nurse training. I recalled that was one thing that my mother had impressed on me not to accept and so I stuck out for the registered nurse place. I did not have the required qualifications at the time but was determined to get them and enrolled for further education at Fod House. I gained my extra qualifications there and took up my place eventually to train as a registered nurse.

Fod house was a further education establishment which was situated on a previous farmland and was the precursor to Lauder college.

 I would never have believed many years later I would enter Lauder College as a lecturer in Healthcare, Socialcare and Childcare.

My colleagues at the hospital were cock a hoop for me as was my family and to be honest I was fairly chuffed myself as I was the third nurse in my family to start their nurse training but the first to do registered nursing.

I was due to start my training in the September of 1977 and although I would miss my colleagues I was looking forward to moving into a whole new world and more importantly gain a room and bed of my own.

I had shared my bed and bedroom with 1-4 siblings for most of my life and it was not something I was going to miss. Much as I loved my sisters it was difficult manoeveres at night with 4 in the bed. If one turned you all had to turn. My younger sister flailed in her sleep as she was quite restless but the worst was when she wet the bed. Then it was four groggy sisters all out to change the bedding and ourselves.

Generally speaking in 1977 in the country it was the Queens jubilee year, the firemen went on strike the same year (I became fully aware of this in my first placement just a few months down the line) more later.

The country was hit with star wars fever and the punk rock group sex pistols hit the airwaves as punk music took off with this anarchist group. Its music which was a mix of punk fashion and anarchic politics which set youngsters on fire with a passion. The youth felt they had found a rebellion to join. The parents and monarchists failed to discover or place who this group were or what their purpose was in the scheme of things. Apart from making a din and spreading dissatisfaction amongst the disaffected youth.

I was more into Donny Osmond, Gilbert O'Sullivan and the Bay City Rollers myself.

Chapter two –

College – Characters & Friends

College was interesting and informative and the tutors were in a league of their own as they tried, some less successful than others to pass on the wisdom and knowledge we would need to become competent nurses.

I was delighted to move into the nurse's home as it was the first time I had both a bed of my own and a room of my own and even though the room was only twelve feet by eight feet I thought being able to lock my own door was paradise.

I was in a group of 40 other would be nurses and was one of the 4 Lorna's which was quite a surprise as I had been the only Lorna in my high school of a thousand students. It was interesting to note that of the 4 Lorna's I was the only one who qualified.

Our tutors were certainly from a dying breed of nurses who were used to the hierarchical system of nursing to task and being handmaidens to the doctors who often enjoyed an elevated and reverential position.

I was asked at one point in a very busy surgical ward if I would go and get the bone china tea service out and make the consultant a pot of tea. When I declined to do so, the look of horror at my insubordination on the ward Sisters face, nearly made me change my mind.

Some of our lessons were an absolute hoot, such as when Mr Rhodes, our lecturer, a tall and upright man of almost sargeant major bearing, demonstrated how to do a sterile dressing.

He spoke with an extremely broad Fife accent which was usually blasted at about 85 decibels. Looking back I think he must have been partially deaf as he was a nice man. He may have had the bearing of an army man but with his bottle end thick glasses and clumsy demeanor, made him appear quite comical.

Preparation he shouted and sprayed is the key to a good dressing and when his dog's dinner of a trolley was demonstrated, we tried not to look with disdain.   The piece de resistance was when he demonstrated how to open these new fangled sterile packs and sent the contents flying across the floor. We stifled our laughter.

Recovering his composure and speaking in a broad dialect noo yoo lassies will no hae that problem as this is an old pack, as he then scraped the contents off the floor.

It was the least sterile dressing I have ever seen and a clear cut case of do as I tell you not as you see.

He was also the tutor who taught us how to undertake cardio pulmonary resuscitation (CPR)which seemed to be a very useful skill to learn. The lessons were progressing well and the theory fairly straightforward but unfortunately we were unable to practice the skills as the dummy was broken.

Never mind lassies cos maist nurses never come across a cardiac arrest in their career, said Mr Rhodes which in my case was a misplaced statement.

Fears allayed then as we were allocated our ward to practice our new found skills on real live patients. We were kitted out in our dress uniforms and paper caps and I was sent with one of my colleagues to the surgical ward.

I was absolutely petrified at the thought of being let loose with brand new skills in a fast faced surgical ward with lots of people calling me nurse and asking for things with names which sounded distinctly foreign to me.

However as we attempted to do the temperatures pulses and respiratory observations of the patients, I heard a strangled cry of the medical student behind the curtain calling for help. I gingerly popped my head around the screen to hear the medical student squeak out help me this man has arrested.

 Jings a real heart attack and would I help her, me a student nurse who had never even taken a temperature never mind assist a man whose heart had ceased beating.

As I desperately thought what to do, my flight or fight reflex kicked in and my mouth involuntarily spoke the words, you do the compressions and I will go and get help and come back to help you. I then darted out to the corridor and bliss, happened upon a trained nurse and blurted out that a man has arrested in the bay can you come and help, she gave me a bewildered look and walked briskly away.

At this point I was breathing faster and panicking inwardly for the man who seemed destined to die through our incompetence. Fortunately a brave third year student nurse approached and I explained quickly and she said she would call the crash team. I then went back to help with my limited skills and inexperience, to a medical student who by this time was sobbing as she tried to do CPR.

I moved forward to remove the back of the bed to allow me to do the mouth to mouth part of the CPR. Right at this point I seemed to fly through the air as the crash team arrived and bodily pushed me out of the way.

Once I had just about composed myself and realised why I had just gained the gift of flight, a patient from the bed opposite the man who had arrested looked at me and said, yer no bloody doin that tae me. He then proceeded to rip out his intravenous cannula and with blood pouring out of his arm legged it out of the ward with the words I'm going tae Edinburgh.

Just as my mind was composing the phrase what a madness the charge nurse shouted at me after him nurse McQueen. It was a never ending nightmare.

However I survived and went back to college partly in shell shock and partly confused by the whole situation but the caring sharing NHS came to the fore with the a debrief session the next day when Mr Rhodes stated in the passing, heard you had an interesting day yesterday Nurse McQueen. That was the sum total of the debrief.

Well one of the things this episode told me was if I was ever going to be put off nursing it would have been at this point so I had the mettle it would seem to undertake the rigours of the profession.

I was already used to the early starts of a dayshift as I had done a milk delivery round with my dad, starting at 04.00am. It was a nightmare, dad would start off gently telling me it was time to get up and dressed, my brother Harry came too. However our mecurial dad and his volcanic temper was quickly displayed when we didn't mind read dads instructions for the milk orders or which doors we were to deliver to. He would just yell fkin take 2 pints there, he then angrily pointed to an area that had several houses. We would be asking timidly through flowing tears, which number? fkin run now he shouted. We would be running blindly to a door we guessed at and hoped for the best. Its comical now as I describe it but then it was agony. I still recall old ladies coming up to us on the round to give us a smile and a sweetie as they clearly felt sorry for us. If only dad had controlled his temper and said take two pints to number 22 all would have been well. He must have woken the whole street with his histrionics, I bet they loved having him as a milkman.

Chapter Three

Surgeons & Surgical Cases

I have to admit being a student nurse in the late seventies was both scary and exhilarating, yet I was one of the most enthusiastic student nurses you could wish to find. As I felt every shift was an adventure in waiting and I needed to be in early to start the exploration.

I recall being on duty in the surgical ward at least half an hour early and was going round the ward checking to see what patients were in and what stage of recovery the patients were at in their treatment.

 I was taking notes to inform myself what needs to be done when I noticed that one of the drips had run through and needed changing.

I had retrieved the necessary infusion and was just about to start changing the bag when I was startled by an auxillary roaring down the ward at me what do you think you are doing. I replied that I was going to change the infusion that was run through just leave it she snarled that is my job.

I was both intimidated and annoyed but acquiesced and moved on. It was in the days when auxillary nurses on night duty often ruled the roost and were a law unto themselves. Some were very good and some were a menace and all without formal training.

In the days before the second world war a good auxillary could advance to enrolled nurse level and senior enrolled nurse level without formal training and qualifications, which seems extraordinary when you consider the onus on training and qualifications now.

I loved the buzz of the surgical wards and the fast pace and seemingly high turnover of the post operative patients who had surgery with us in the general hospital. If required they were then sent to the Hunter hospital to convalesce.

What I wasn't so fond of was the smell of putrid flesh caused by all manner of bacteria. To this day I would be able to step into any ward and without going anywhere near a patient be able to tell if someone had gas gangrene in their wound. I could also identify by smell a black tarry stool called melena , caused by bleeding in the gut or trauma in the body or simply due to diet such as eating black licorice, on ingesting iron tablets.

However often the extreme smelling melena stools warrant investigation as they may signal bleeding in the gut.

In the 1970s and 1980s hospital stays were much longer than now, for instance if you had an appendicectomy you stayed in hospital on average 5-7 days and for a cholestotectomy (removal of gall bladder) it was 10-14 days. In the 21st century you can have a hip replacement as a day patient so go in for 08.00 hours and be home for 18.00 hours the same day. Unheard of in my day but what a change which in so many ways were still way ahead of my understanding.

The next day after the stomach churning CPR incident, we went back to the surgical ward and I was introduced to an elderly, emaciated lady with a bloated abdomen. A much younger man was with her and I assumed to be her son and whom over the course of the time I knew them, seemed to be devoted to his mother.
It was lovely to see his devotion as it was apparent even to me that his mother was seriously ill and indeed upon enquiring I discovered that she was not expected to last a few more days as her liver cancer was very advanced.

It was indeed just two days later when I came into the ward and noticed that her space was empty to be informed that she had died through the night in a most distressing scene for all involved.

Her husband whom I had thought to be her son was overcome with emotion and was distraught and had to be literally pulled off her body to allow the undertakers to care for his wife.

The full story was revealed to me at this point and it transpired that this old lady was in fact a young woman of twenty six years old and had become unwell on her honeymoon just three months previously and the couple had cut the holiday short to fly home to the devastating news that Sharon had Liver cancer and it was already advanced and spread throughout her body with no hope of a cure and a prognosis of 3-6 months.

Her husband Bill had to play a secondary role of companion and his bright future with the woman he loved, cruelly cut short. No wonder the man was distraught; life can be so cruel sometimes.

As a student nurse we were only learning as we went along and our experience was limited which led me to make some dreadful conclusions such as in the case of the middle aged lady who was noisy and becoming a nuisance to the other women in the six bay area. This lady was admitted with severe abdominal pain but was complaining more and more of headaches and up until this point the surgeons had been unable to find out what was wrong with her. I was approached by one of the other ladies in the bay and asked if I would have a word with this lady as the rest of the women found her strange noises unsettling and disturbing their sleep. In my efficiency and can do manner I boldly approached the lady and told her in an assertive manner just how she was upsetting others and would she kindly stop it. Well job done I thought and went about doing good for others safe in the knowledge that I was fast becoming a brisk and efficient surgical nurse. What I did not reckon on was that instead of giving the woman a talking to I should have thought more deeply about what was causing her to behave in this manner and discussed this with one of the senior nurses or doctors. I was to learn to my shame that this lady was finally diagnosed with an inoperable brain tumour and that was causing the strange behaviours.

Although I did report the strange but I am convinced true information to the staff nurses of a curious case with a patient. Jim a young post operative man confided in me one day his worries about his health. Jim was aged twenty seven and single, unemployed and had just had his appendix removed. When I went into his room to answer his call bell he was still a wee bit groggy from his operation and anaesthesia and he beckoned me to him so he could tell me something. I bent down to hear him tell me that he was worried that he thought his sperm was going to go green. I asked him what made him think this and he told me that as he was lonely and had no girlfriend so he was making love to his dog and hence the worry about his sperm. Well at this point my facial expression must have moved from neutral passive to perturbed concern as he said you think I'm weird eh? Well I certainly do not think it is normal to be having sex with a dog even if you are lonely and left it at that.

It was only years later when reading the story of Papillion and his escapades on trying to escape from the French penal system did i realise that this was not a new phenomenon.

I was once again quite glad of my sheltered upbringing with regards to sex and drugs, and amazed at the colourful life nursing was opening up to me.

It was a mixed surgical ward I was working in and the charge nurse was lovely if a bit manic and had huge feet. Sister Brown often rushed about as if the ward was on fire and forgot to take breakfast and would occasionally drop in a faint with low blood sugars, I was quite alarmed the first time I witnessed this but the other nurses were so used to her doing this then recovering on her own that they just said never mind her she will be ok and just stepped over her and got on with their own work. She was a very fine ward sister and kind to me and her staff.

I recall working with my colleague Lynn who was always inadvertently putting her foot in it. For instance when we were doing a wound dressing for a middle aged man who had an incision and drain from a haematoma on his scrotum following a vasectomy. Lynn and I went into the room together and were chatting gaily with this man in a bid to diffuse his embarrassment about working on his private parts. So far so good until Lynn came out with the classic, you know its such a shame you have had such a bother it being such a small thing. The man had gone a bright shade of red when Lynn realised that the man thought she was making derogatory remarks about his manhood when she meant minor surgery. We quickly finished the dressing and I bundled Lynn out of the room before she dug herself deeper but we did chuckle at her faux pas but I'm not so sure the man did.

story in Scots dialect of a wee boy chatting away excitedly with his parents as they head to his grandparents in Kirkcaldy on the train.

The Boy in the Train;

Whit way does the engine say "Toot-toot"

Is it feart to gang in the tunnel?

Whit wey is the furnace no pit oot

When the rain gangs doon the funnel?

What'll I hae for my tea the nicht?

A herrin', or maybe a haddie?

Has Granma gotten electric licht?

Is the next stop Kirkcaldy?

There's a hoodie craw on yon turnip raw

An seagulls sax or seven

I'll no fa oot o' the windae, Maw

Its sneckit, as sure as I'm leevin

We're in the tunnel! We're a' in the dark!

But dinna be frichtit Daddy,

We'll sune be comin' to Beveridge Park

And the next stop's Kirkcaddy!

Is yon a mune I see in the sky?

It's awfu wee an curly

See! Theres a coo and a cauf ootbye,

An a lassie pu'in a hurly

He's chackit the tickets and gien them back,

Sae gie me my ain yin, Daddy

Lift doon the bag frae the luggage rack,

For the next stop's Kirkcaddy!

There's a gey when boats at the harbour mou',

And eh! Dae ye see the cruisers?

The cinnamon drop I was sookin the noo

Has tummelt an' stuck tae ma troosers…

I'll sune be ringin' ma Gran'ma's bell,

She'll cry, "Come ben, my laddie',

For I ken mysel' by the queer like smell

That the next stop's Kirkcaddy!

M.C Smith.

I worked in at least 5 of these cottage hospitals and each of them had

a very different feel but all were memorable in different ways.

The Northern in Dunfermline; 1843- 1980

It started life as the poorhouse for those destitute people to go as a place of last resort prior to the inauguration of the welfare state. You did not luxuriate in a workhouse as you were set to work immediately unless you were sick.

Jobs were allocated to inmates from splitting wood for the men to laundry for the women. The trustees felt that work, regardless if you were missing a limb was imperative to keep inmates contented.

They do have a point as lack of structure and purpose in a day can frustrate and cause harm to your mental well being.

However even the derogatory title of inmates, to the segregation of families must have caused much more mental turmoil. The shame and disgrace of having to go to the poorhouse is well documented in history.

The Northern Hospital was upgraded in the 1950s for the care of the chronic sick.

I worked there in 1976 and recall it was at the end of a lane next door to a cemetery and at night after a late shift walking back along the lane felt a bit spooky. The lane was not well lit and as I was a teenager the thought of the poor souls who existed and died in the place gave me the shivers.

I worked as explained in the first floor geriatric ward and asked to be shown the sleeping quarters of the inmates. I squeezed up a narrow and low ceilinged staircase and was shown a small attic area with one tiny window. It was dark gloomy and oppressive and housed upwards of 50 people, talk about close fellowship. That's why I said folks within existed, as the life of the poorhouse was horrid, albeit it kept the destitute off the streets. If you ever want to read more about the life of folks in the times of the poorhouses, I highly recommend the Ragged Trousered Philanthropist by Robert Tressell.

I felt the vibes of the history of the building when working in the Northern but enjoyed my time there. It was sold to a private company in 1980 and has been used as a nursing home for the elderly since.

Stratheden Hospital; 1866- present

It was known as Fife and Kinross district asylum and in 1948 at the inauguration of the NHS it was incorporated as Stratheden Hospital. It is based in beautiful countryside by Cupar and is known for being a centre of excellence in child and family psychiatry. As with all asylums they were placed away from the main hubbub of a town as the shame and stigma of mental illness was prevalent then. It is much better now but still the stigma lingers, though that is improving with time and education.

It is strange how we fear what we cannot comprehend or see, yet one in four of us will have mental health issues at any given time.

In my time there as a student nurse my perception was of a place that provided some good some bad and some indifferent care. I found the staff and patients to be institutionalised and wondered why on earth anyone should be subjected to such poor care.

There were two scales, one set of staff worked 8am to 1pm and the next distinct group worked 1pm till 8 pm, then the nightshift took over. The staff on the different scales had very different ideas of how the wards and treatment should be run and work distributed.

No wonder the patient care was patchy and patient progress slow or so it seemed to me. There was no real consistency in care planning and it seemed like a competition to make your mark.

The staff I worked with were friendly on the whole but many were often as institutionalised as the patients. There seemed to be a lot of affairs among staff and I will explain later, regarding the charge nurse trying to hit on to me.

I once tried to divert an old man with a shuffling gait into another ward as I knew he was not one of our patients. I had my hand on his elbow when he mumbled something I found hard to decipher, when the aforementioned charge nurse shouted down to me.

I see you have met Dr Sharp, Nurse McQueen. I had not and with a puzzled look tried to locate the person she was talking about when the mumbling man told me that was him! Oh my word, well I was staggered that this old gentleman who I mistook for one of the patients was a Consultant psychiatrist. I just thought thank goodness I am mentally well at this time and do not require the use of his services.

Craigtoun Maternity Hospital; 1948-1992

I loved my time residing in Craigtoun maternity hospital when I was a student at Stratheden hospital. Its grandeur and elegance were just stunning even though its heyday had passed and its days as a hospital were numbered.

It was originally contained within the Mount Melville estate, which was established in1695 for General Robert Melville of Strathkinnes. He developed the grounds and planted over 230 trees to create a beautiful parkland and it is still growing well today.

 In 1901 The brewing family of Dr James Younger took ownership and commissioned Waterhouse architects to design a new mansion house and add to the landscaping. It is a large Edwardian free style house with a skyline of gables, conical and facetted roofed turrets. It has retaining walls and wrought iron gates.

It has the most beautiful alabaster and marble elegantly sweeping staircase. I was bowled over when I first saw it and could easily imagine ladies in their evening attire being escorted down these stairs by suitably sartorially dressed gentleman.

A girl can dream and absorb the vibes of history and tales a house can emanate.

Our bedrooms were of grand proportions which took my breath away, especially since I had lived in council or army houses most of my life until then.

On its conversion to a maternity hospital it housed 40 expectant mothers. At the time I was in residence in the 1970's it had an unsympathetic extension added for the use of 31 geriatric patients. It felt like we had the run of the house and we all felt very much at home.

Certainly one of my classmates an Australian girl felt so at home I distinctly remember her delight and noises, at bathing with her boyfriend in the grand bathroom. She was one of the students who did not pass her end exams, no surprise given her other preoccupations.

As Craigtoun was a distance from Stratheden hospital, my colleagues and I were picked up each morning in a minivan, driven by a lovely farmers wife whose second job was driving us to Stratheden.

It was such a treat to be taken all the back roads of the countryside near St Andrews to go to work and to be taught the rudiments of driving by her as we went along.

On a weekend shift at Stratheden I recall the pleasure of taking in the beauty of the countryside and then the joy of a civilised start to our shift by a full cooked breakfast laid out on a long table like a feast for a king.

Only once we had consumed our fill in a leisurely manner did we rise to care for our patients.

Hunter Hospital; 1936-1992

It had been gifted to the NHS by John Hunter (1831-1916). He was a native of Kirkcaldy and a prominent citizen, who became the Dean of the Guild of the Burgh. On his death he gifted his beautiful home to the NHS for the poor and incurables who could not afford to be treated at home.

It was in this same ward that I met a very interesting manic depressive when she was in her manic phase. As I explained earlier lots of the staff and patients in this institution were institutionalised. Holistic and individual care were in the future as I shouted to the patients to line up and collect their pills from me in my drug trolley in the middle of the ward.

The bulk of the ladies shuffled, walked and resignedly came to form an orderly queue beside me when Ruth who at five feet ten and weighing in at a healthy fourteen stone skipped up beside me singing a lovely ditty. As she towered above me and blocked out much of my view and the sunlight as she beamed down at me and said in a falsetto tone. If you try to give me any pills I will shove them along with that spoon right past your teeth and down your throat, ok. Well that was enough reason for me and I excused her from pills for the day, at least from me. Ruth smiled sweetly at me and skipped away singing her sweet tunes.

However it is at the most peculiar times that you begin to realise that the world is indeed a small place as when I was called to attend an emergency section where a woman of my age was being forcibly taken into care for her own protection under the mental health act.

I was always excited to being part of something new in my repertoire of nursing firsts and enjoyed the discussion of the possible restraint procedures that may be needed and the medication that was prescribed if required. It seemed no time until the ambulance pulled up at a house and I went in behind my colleagues to a scene of mayhem.

A distraught family were trying to calm down a hysterical young woman who was bleeding from lacerations on her wrist and who had already swallowed numerous pills in an attempt to take her life. I was so caught up in trying to assimilate the entire goings on of the emergency team and witnessing the distress of this young woman that it took me a while to realise that this was one of my school friends. It must have dawned on her at the same time and the realisation added to her distress, and I felt for her.

Life seems to move so slowly when you are younger and it is only with hindsight that as an older person you begin to realise the magnitude of the life you lived as a youth and did not fully appreciate it. Or just maybe the rose tinted spectacles you wear nostalgically really are rosy. It did seem like a dream when I look back on my youth and the people I met and friends I shared my life with.

mind to avoid blemishing the family and society) as one of our first student nurse placements. We were posted initially to the Craigton hospital nurses home, set out in the country of the East Neuk of Fife. It was a beautiful mansion house that had belonged to the Younger family who made their money in the brewing industry. I remember the first time I entered by the front entrance and viewed the grand spiral marble staircase, I stood and gazed with awe as my mind sought to replicate the grand evenings when the house would prepare itself for the arrival of invited guests to a ball and the hosts would glide regally down the wonderful staircase to receive them in their beautifull ballgowns and tuxedos. I seemed to have arrived at the end of an era and was caught up in a changing of the guard ceremony when the NHS was moving from a world of cottage hospitals and paternal benificance to one of cutting edge technology and beaurocratic organisation.

Although I saw the need for change a bit of me yearned for part of the status quo to remain.

We worked hard and enjoyed all our experiences of mental health and certainly enjoyed having to transfer patients from Stratheden to the general hospital for any medical or surgical investigations. On one occasion I recall after dropping our patient at the General hospital the paramedics asked if I was in a rush to get back to work or if I fancied a wee tour of the countryside and a coffee stop at a local café. It took me a nanosecond to be persuaded and I spent the next couple of hours taking in the delights of the east Fife countryside.

I could never imagine getting away with that nowadays. Such simple pleasures bring immeasurable joy.

We were a fine mix of student colleagues, me who was delighted to see the world beyond my small town and have my own bedroom. Avril the diminutive blonde who was engaged to the tall and handsome Richard, Jerry the Aussie who was loud and brash and very much liked the men. Margaret a fiery redhead who was bold and self assured and lastly Rosalind who was quiet, beautiful and a real giggler. We had such fun as students getting to know each other, exchanging reminiscences and venturing into the local town and tea shop on our wee mopeds.

The cafe was a lovely quaint tea shop inhabited by old ladies, who dressed in their fur coats and hats and met for a gentile day out. They would be relaxing for a wee blether, so when we motor bikers came breezing into their habitat, many worried facial expressions and exchanges rapidly followed. The silence and looks of initial disdain was going to be in a bit of bother. I was to go directly to the matrons office which I did in trepidation and anxiety. I knocked and popped my head round the door and the chief fireman (who defied the strike to attend the fire) and matron were waiting for me. The fire chief asked if I was nurse McQueen and that was I the person who had extinguished the fire. I confirmed I was and he then commended me for my level head and skill in dealing with a fat fire which could have caused a great deal of damage. I accepted the praise sheepishly and went to work in the ward and never let on that not only did I extinguish it I had started it with my absent mindedness.

Chapter 5 –

Womens trouble's

I was by now in the field of gynaecology a specialty I thoroughly enjoyed and to which I gained my first post as a staff nurse. The ward was run by a very old school charge nurse Miss Douglas who ran a very ship shape ward. It was run on almost military lines and the staff and Doctors were all afraid to put a foot wrong in her ward. However she was a fair if firm charge nurse and all she did was for the benefit of the patients. When I arrived in the ward Miss Douglas had been in charge for nearly two decades and was still utilising treatments and procedures that had proved their worth for over thirty years.

Although now when you mention some of them to newer nurses they squirm and scorn at the practices we used.

 Yet they worked very well and were of great help to the patients in the era they were used in and I often think the phrase not scientific enough or evidence based fails to not give credence to the years of experiential proven use.

Some of them included giving milk and treacle enemas for post operations involving the use of carbon dioxide to push the pelvic organs out of the way, a common post -operative complaint by women is extreme pain caused by the retained gas.

The milk and treacle enema was a wonderful gentle way of sorting this problem out and many thousands of women were grateful for the help and relief this provided.

However in this day and age of evidence based practice this treatment seemed unscientific and given no trials were carried out to prove its efficacy, it was ditched in favour of such things as flatus tubes and peppermint water, which were of limited use.

We also used treatments such as egg white and oxygen on excoriated skin which proved to be a great healer but again with the scares of salmonella and unscientific use we once again threw the baby out with the bathwater.

Gynaecology was a fast paced ward with emergency admissions and theatre days making it exciting, busy and often heavy for the nursing staff.

The saddest group of people I nursed on this ward were those women who were going for surgery following the diagnosis of ovarian cancer. They were often middle aged women with their families in their late teens or early twenties. At this time in their lives were fully immersed in the hustle and bustle of family life while maintaining a job and heading towards the menopause.

The surgery I often found in my limited perception, hastened the end for these women as it seemed to spread the dreadful disease.

Ovarian cancer was often referred to as the silent killer, as its symptoms of bowel changes and abdominal discomfort and swelling were often put down to "the change" or middle age.

(If you are ever worried about any of the conditions I talk about reader, do chat with your GP or visit the NHS website as it has very useful information. Whatever you do don't try Google, go to the experts.)

Then when it was finally diagnosed the disease was usually spread throughout the body and really too late for treatment.

I found chatting with these women to be a very difficult balancing act between being reassuring to these worried women, while silently harbouring the knowledge of their impending doom.

young woman who came into the ward from the street and marched up to nurses station and told me she wanted some confidential information and she needed it right away.

I asked her how old she was as she held me eye to eye without shame or embarrassment beside her wee pal who was squirming beside her. I'm just gone thirteen but you've to keep this a secret, I slept with my boyfriend and think I may be pregnant. Now will you give me the morning after pill or do I have to go to my doctor?! In some ways it was good that this young girl knew where to come and had the confidence to ask for assistance. I would have been sad if any of my daughters were having such emotional turmoil from such a young age. I always wanted my children to remain children for as long as possible so they could enjoy childhood and innocence before the stresses of adulthood beckoned.

I also met a remarkable older lady in the gynaecology ward, of the older generation who are both stoical and incredibly steeped in their traditional cultural values. So much so that they put up with things that our current generations would not dream of doing.

Mrs Rennie was a 78 year old lady who had come in for a hysterectomy and I was asked to admit her, I introduced myself to her and smiled at this very proper but sweet looking lady whose dress was immaculate and whose demeaner was shy and unassuming.

I noticed immediately a dreadful smell coming from her direction which seemed at odds with her attire and since the smell was nearly overwhelming I had to try hard to not show any disdain at the smell which somehow was coming from her.

I discovered she was a married lady who had two daughters and three adult grandchildren who seemed to be very fond of their grandmother.

Mrs Rennie lived in a bungalow in the town with her husband of fifty five years and was fairly fit and independent. However when she got changed and into her nightdress she showed me with embarrassment and not a little reluctance the reason for the smell and her need for hysterectomy.

Mrs Rennie had a total prolapse of her uterus and it transpired that this appendage, for all intense purposes looked like a large rotting cauliflower. It was her womb with numerous growths that had become cancerous which was causing the smell.

The amazing thing was that she told me that this had prolapsed when she was thirty eight years of age and she had been walking about with this appendage between her legs for forty years.

I was incredulous and asked her what did her husband think about this as she was a married lady and all intimate relations would have ceased the day it prolapsed. She replied oh we did not like to talk about women's things like that and just kept it quiet.

This business of keeping things quiet nearly ended the life of the young woman who was admitted to the gynaecology ward, barely conscious and literally pouring pus from her vagina.

We discovered that her and her partner had thought it might be good fun to use a can of hairspray into their repertoire of sex toys and inserted this device during foreplay. However when withdrawing the canister the lid came off and it was stuck inside her.

Now since they realised that the use of this device was neither conventional or advocated by many for fun and indeed may make them an article of ridicule. They decided in their wisdom to let things be and leave it to find its own way out.

Of course that was a foolish proposition and the bodies reaction to foreign objects is to try and consume them and eradicate them but it could not break down the plastic top and her body was overwhelmed.

The infection was by now rampant and indeed she was septicaemic and a very ill woman. Fortunately the cap was removed surgically as was her uterus and any means now of becoming a mother, a tragic end to a "bit of fun".

Chapter 6-

Medical Macinations

I then moved onto the medical ward and came under the care of the diminutive but quietly powerful charge nurse Miss Farmer. Like my friend Avril, Miss Farmer would be lucky if she reached five foot in height. Although what she lacked in inches she gained fully in respect and admiration from all her staff as she was a lovely lady and very much in charge of her ward.

I will never forget the way she dealt with medical students and junior Doctors who had the temerity to ignore her rules for tidy up as you go. A lot of medical staff at that time expected the nurses to become their handmaiden and tidy up their mess.

Come with me nurse McQueen, Sister Farmer called. I was wee bit worried as all students are a wee bit paranoid when summoned by the ward sister and always wondered if they had done something wrong.

I need not have worried as she called two medical students who at six feet plus towered above the two of us to follow her and pay attention to what she demonstrated to them. The medical students came quietly and without question given the authoritative tone used in the request. We were all led to the dishevelled bed of a lady the students had examined earlier. Now gentlemen please pay attention to the way Nurse McQueen and I make this bed and observe the hospital corners. Once we had completed the task Sister Farmer asked the students to remake the bed in the same fashion we had done and asked if they now felt competent in the task. To which they replied quite meekly yes thank you sister. Lesson learned, they tidied up after themselves from that day hence.

We were now second year student nurses and many of our group were either engaged or dating men who were to become our husbands and very much enjoying our nursing and lives in general.

In the late seventies there were not many men in nursing and my experience of the ones I came across were that they were either quite effeminate or were lazy, often a bit weedy and wanted an easy life as they saw it, in mental health. Paul was one of those in the latter category and he was also very handsome and for all intense purposes looked like he should have been a lumberjack. I have worked with many excellent men in nursing since. (I do dislike the title male nurse it just seems odd, they are nurses yes but why is it prefixed with their gender, just saying.)

When we worked together on the medical ward it was very heavy and busy work, so all hands were needed on deck to make the work lighter. Especially in the task orientated days, we started with giving patients bedbaths and making their beds, before moving to observations.

I remember one day being run off my feet and looking for help from Paul but could not find him and eventually knocked on the toilet door and asked if he was in there. He replied he was and could I just leave him to read his paper for a wee while and then he would help me in the ward with the patients. Get your lazy backside out of there just now you wee besom I sternly said through gritted teeth. Which he did quite unperturbed and ambled out to help me in his laconic and cheerful manner. He was a lovely man really and went into mental health nursing after his general nurse training. He became a charge nurse and was doing well until his marriage broke up, that was when he took to the drink. I had not heard about him for a while and met up with him a few years later when he had aged considerably and had lost his looks and the last I heard of him was that he was found dead aged forty outside his bed-sit. He had been trying to get in the window as he had lost his key after a drunken night out and had fallen asleep on the pavement and choked on his own vomit. It was the sad end to a lovely and promising young man, such a waste as the demon drink pulled another lost soul into the abyss.

In the world at large the prime minister of Rhodesia Ian Smith had just agreed with three black leaders, one of whom became a notorious tyrant to take over the rule of the country. The Premiers mantle was handed to Robert Mugabe as at the time the British government felt it was too risky to support and back Nkono the opposition leader. Oh what an error of judgement and turmoil they caused for the country for many decades due to their meddling.

They agreed for Robert Mugabe to take the lead in the handover to black majority rule in what is now Zimbabwe.

Mugabe may have started off with good intentions, a man who had been a school teacher and nurturer but quickly changed to become a power mad megalomaniac. He took the breadbasket of Africa to the basket case of that continent and to this day the country has not recovered.

The population of the world was a third less at just over 4 billion, Sony had introduced the revolutionary walkman a portable stereo system and the Deer Hunter was a smash at the box office. The Watergate scandle within the Presidency of Richard Nixon was unfolding and eventually toppled his administration.

However when you are a young woman these world politics seem to skiff over you as you concentrate on and remember the important things like the walkman and the music such as Fleetwood Macs album rumors with the sexy song in it.

Chapter 7

Students Reunion

It was lovely going back to college after our placements and meet up again with all our classmates and find out who was doing what and who had left.

I always enjoyed returning to college and looking forward to lectures in a new subject. It was back to a surgical block this time and lectures with the consultant surgeon Mr Drumley.

He was a tall imposing man who was at the twilight of his career and was quite eccentric. Lectures usually consisted of typical and atypical surgical complaints and the anatomical and physiological reasons for them, with associated nursing care.

However with Mr Drumley although he taught us all about common surgical complaints and associated anatomy he also taught us how to actually perform operations and how to suture and provide post operative care.

The first time it happened in class when he asked us what type of suture we liked to use we looked back bemused but when he blustered come now what type do you use we just answered the same as you Sir, good good he replied, happy that order was restored.

It was only a couple of years later that we heard this very fine surgeon was suffering from dementia and being nursed in the mental health hospital that we had worked in as student nurses.

It just goes to show you that death disease and dying are no respecter of persons and that it is important to live by the maxim Carpe Diem. Since if we do not seize each day and make the most of each opportunity we may just run out of time and opportunity.

All too soon we were back into the wards trying to keep up with placement work and providing the college with the necessary academic requirements needed to pass each section in our training. As well as integrate into a new area and field of nursing, it was all new and exciting for us and many lifelong friendships were made and developed in a shared pursuit.

We had quite a few male tutors in college who were kindly men who encouraged us in our studies. I recall Mr freeman who decided to use my case study of a patient I had worked with who had Downs Syndrome as an exemplar. He extolled to the class how well it was written and what a lovely relationship I had with the young man. He said it was clear the time effort and energy I had taken with getting to grips with this syndrome and care required within the case study. He said how clear my work had allowed this young man to thrive.

It was amazing to hear such glowing terms about my knowledge and skills as unknown to Mr Freeman I had cobbled the case study together the day before based on a mix of knowledge learned and patients nursed previously. My friends and I all knew this and so I was ribbed mercilessly by them.

We were reunited in the main general hospital in the fine town of Kirkcaldy and given rooms in the tower block of a nursing home with Miss Elford the matron as the resident nurse in charge of the home as well.

It was lovely to be back in touch with all my friends as I had missed them and looked forward to catching up with all the gossip and what was happening in their lives. It was also a time to become friendlier with others in our class like Susan a tall, elegant and beautiful young woman who told us she was in love with Steve her boyfriend but was not sure if he loved her.

It was certainly a case of does he does he not that seemed to enter into every conversation we had and I felt it was time to take the bull by the horns so when Steve next phoned the communal phone in the nurse's home I took the call. Hi Steve its Lorna you don't know me but I am friends with your girlfriend Susan. Hi Lorna how are you he replied with the passive enquiry of someone who just wants to be put onto his girlfriend. Listen Steve I am going to ask you something and I want you to answer truthfully as this is for your benefit as well. Sounds intriguing should I be worried? Not at all I replied, but tell me do you love Susan? Eh why do you ask?, Well since she loves you and is always worrying if you love her is it not about time you told her and get the marriage proposal organised?

To say Steve was flabbergasted was an understatement but give him his due he shaped up and told her he loved her and indeed they were engaged at the shake of a lambs tale and of course I was invited to their wedding.

Then there was Ruth and Joan who were a bundle of fun and who would never but never be seen out without makeup on and who as time passed developed a desire to marry and work with Arabs. I'm not sure where this interest arose from as there were not a lot of Arabs around in Fife at that time. However the emirates eventually called on them and they spent a great deal of their career fulfilling both of their objectives.

 To someone to whom make up was a curious thing to do I used to find their dread of being seen without their slap really funny. Yet one day I called really early for Ruth and a strange looking lady answered the door, when I asked for Ruth she slapped my arm and told me to stop being silly. I could not believe the difference as Ruth was almost albino and looked incredibly pale and uninteresting but she was still Ruth and a great friend.

The mention of no Arabs in Fife at the time my friends were student nurses reminds me of when my youngest siblings were quite small. We were out walking down the high street in Cowdenbeath when two black men run across the road. My wee brother and sister had looks of incredulity on their faces as they had never seen a black man before as they were very uncommon in Fife at that time. Turning to our mother they shouted as children do and said look mummy chocolate men.

I digress so back to the nurses home and college. As I explained previously when at college we stayed at the nurses home in Kirkcaldy. This was a tall 1960 block building which each corridor had a kitchen, living room, bathroom and bedrooms. Nothing flash or exciting and certainly not like the exacting standards of today with en-suite facilities, wifi and the latest gadgetry installed within. It felt homely to us and we had a fine time meeting at the end of the day to discuss any issues, new learning or new skills.

Rosalind was now married to her beloved Jim and was ecstatic to realise that now only did she bag Jim and his E type jaguar but that his parents were rich as well and it seemed to spark a very long run of good fortune for them. Jims mum sent Rosalind a cheque every month until they were married to help her save for the wedding. Then gave them a five thousand deposit for their first house as well as the collection of solid silver racing car ingots which were worth a fortune. Indeed it seemed lady luck was certainly favouring them since when they put their deposit down for their house were entered into a prize draw for a free garage extension and of course they won.

Indeed for their first wedding anniversary they were gifted the deeds to a wee cottage in the borders and as Eric and I were married by that time we went as their guests for the weekend to their beautiful cottage which was jam packed with antique furniture. They were living the high life while we were living in a council masionette the poor relations to our lovely rich friends.

Within the nurses home there were brand new students like us through to our senior students who were nearly qualified and about to look for their first posts as staff nurses and enter the profession in fear and anticipation.

Sandra and Lyndsey were two senior student nurses who were nearly qualified and whom I got to know very well through the nurses Christian fellowship group we formed. I have known them all my adult life and cherished their friendship.

I also worked with both of them, Sandra when she became Charge nurse of the childrens ward and Lyndsey when we were colleagues in the neonatal unit.

Sandra was a worry to me when she would take her hour long baths in the only bathroom on the landing, also as I had to run elsewhere to spend a penny.

Since I was always worried she would drown while sleeping in the bath. I got her to tell me when she was having a bath and then knock on the door to see if she was still in the land of the living. Thankfully she didn't drown and after she met her husband Alan it became his responsibility to ensure her safety. They went to be missionaries in Malawi and I joined them for a couple of short term missions, cherished friends doing excellent work.

Lyndsey was an absolute character and an amazing woman, who had to overcome many major health difficulties from birth, due to her mother contracting Rubella in pregnancy.

She was tall, slim, with a long neck, dark hair and like Mr Rhodes had bottle thick glasses as she had extremely poor eyesight. She was a highly intelligent woman who often played the fool and any pranks she could get away with.

She trained as a midwife and was very good at her job but her eyesight deteriorated in time and by the time she came to work in the neonatal unit beside me was struggling.

I recall on one occasion taking over from her when she was finishing her nightshift when the lights are dimmed within and without. She reported that she thought one of the twins she was looking after might need fed earlier than usual as she was fairly sure she had accidently fed the same twin twice and that the baby had been a wee bit sick. It was easy to trace the stain of vomited milk that Lyndsey couldn't see in the dark.

Unfortunately Lyndsey had to retire from nursing not long after that and within a year of early retirement was given the diagnosis of Motor Neurone disease and a prognosis of less than 2 years. It was so sad that this lovely woman who had dealt so stoically with ill health all her life, never even got 2 years of retirement.

I was an executor of Lyndseys will and she asked for her ashes to be scattered at Loch Morlich. She would have laughed at the sight of us her close friends on a crowded beach area. After a wee prayer I was to trail the ashes from the urn along the beach and Sandra and others were to shield me and cover her ashes with the sand as we went along. It was both sad and funny at the same time, right up Lyndsey's street as she would have laughed at the situation.

Chapter 8 –

Meeting my intended and Paediatrics

I was to meet my husband to be the very same summer as I went off to the Keswick Convention in the Lake District for the bible class camp. I went in the company of two spinsters Margaret and Fay from my church, they drove us down in a cute wee Morris minor. We stayed in a dormitory in Hazelhead Academy in Aberdeen a secondary school, which was closed for the summer. We didn't squat in the premises, it was hired out by the school to generate extra funds during the summer break.

We went every day, afternoon and evening to the church services which did not allow me much time for touritisty things or mingling with other young people. However Margaret and Fay finally told me that I had been invited to a youth group's social evening and they would drop me off, it was to be my introduction to a lifelong friend Evelyn and my husband Eric although more later.

My next stint as a student nurse was in the children's ward in Cameron Hospital which was an infectious diseases hospital and like most hospitals of its kind was set out in the countryside and seemed to exist in a vacuum of its own. The sister of the ward was a very buxom older lady, a sister Johnston who was pleasant, fond of the children but quite fixed in her ways. Her staff had been with her in the ward for several years and were quite regimented as well. There were sixteen beds all in single cubicles to avoid the spread of infections and all with emergency call alarms in the rooms should extra help be required.

I arrived in the ward in the winter during a particularly bad outbreak of whooping cough.

This is a disease which is caused by a highly contagious bacteria called Bordetella Pertussis and is wholly avoidable by immunisation. In the 1970,s when I was in the ward there was a high incidence of over 400,000 cases that year worldwide. This was caused by a drop in parents bringing their children for vaccination due to a scare in side effects of the vaccine.

I was terrified once the sister told me it was vital that I be alert at all times to listen for when a baby cried and to go in and lift the baby and tilt it forward and slap its back to prevent it choking and stopping breathing. My goodness a baby's life in my hands, I can tell you my hearing became supersonic that winter and my sprint speed

woman when I qualified as a midwife as there were no midwifery posts. I was taken on as a staff nurse in the children's ward and she was every bit as scary as my friends had described her to be.

I found her to be lacking in depth as well and on most shifts the key tasks after looking after the children was to keep sister Smart busy in the duty room with chit chat. When I was told it was my turn I was at a loss to know what to talk about and was given the advice that she liked golf and anything related to it. Well there is only so much you can blether about golf courses and Pringles jumpers and so after a pregnant and awkward pause you could not sit and dwell in the uncomfortable silences. I would take my leave from her office and resume duties in the ward.

When I was working with the children in the ward I found them to be very tactile and always looking for a cuddle but I never once saw her hug or pat a child and indeed when a child dared to approach her top lip curled imperceptibly as she told me to keep that child away from her. I found her to be a cold and shallow individual whom I could not warm to at all and even when many people would try and explain her behaviours by implying her coldness may have come from a lost child she endured when younger.

I just could not believe that someone whose life had been touched by tragedy and disappointment would seek a post beside children to snub them.

When she treated me with total lack of empathy after I lost my stillborn child it confirmed my opinion of her that she lacked compassion in her soul. I had come back to work after losing my eldest son to stillbirth at 35 weeks gestation and obviously I was still upset and emotionally raw and coming back to a children's ward. I found it emotionally draining working with lots of babies and toddlers. Making each shift a bit of a slog, it was difficult time for me. So when I was called into her office within the first week back at work I thought she might just be going to extend her sympathies but no the ice maiden explained that a month old baby had just died and since it was so small it would be better if I just carried this dead baby under my nurses cape to the mortuary to save troubling the porter. I still remember thinking at that moment this woman has no compassion or sensitivity and that I would do as asked. Here I was just a few weeks after giving birth to my stillborn baby and now carrying another dead baby close to me. I felt nauseous the whole way and even though it was only a five minute walk it seemed forever as the silent tears rolled down my cheeks which I wiped away just before I handed the dead baby to the mortician.

I remember thinking upon hearing that this charge nurse was finally being moved to another area that it would be a blessing for the children to have a ward sister with more compassion and who actually liked children.

One of the next charge nurses, Sandra was already known to me as a good and lifelong friend and very fine nurse. Interestingly Sandra found Sister Smart to be a valuable help and confidant to her so maybe I misjudged or at least didn't find a way to connect with her. However I did start to feel sorry for the new patients who were going to have to put up with this woman but I need not have worried as she was to become the new theatre sister it was an excellent appointment as all her patients would be unconscious.

We had a lovely time in the nurses home and the girls often had parties in their room trying to keep the noise levels down so not to invoke the "look" and steely admonition from Miss Elford. Indeed we had to keep lookouts for the said Miss Elford if we were trying to sneak friends into our rooms and men were expressly forbidden. All my friends knew I did not drink but were extremely kind and inclusive as they would phone me with an invite with the rejoinder that a pot of tea and bone china cup was being set aside for me. The nurse's home was in the grounds of the hospital and therefore you could wake up five to ten minutes before a shift start and fall into work getting the most sleep possible.

It was expected of the nurses in the nurse's home to respond to every fire alarm and offer their services which was the worst aspect of living as close as there were sixteen flights of stairs.

Indeed I was courting my soon to be fiancé by this time and gauche as I was went to his house to meet him there before being taken out by him for a meal and then he would see me home.

I was always skint and decided that as I was being taken out I would not need any money any way and gaily headed through to East Wemyss the lovely wee mining village where he lived. It was next door to the village that the film Chariots of fire was filmed about the remarkable life of Eric Liddell. However when I got to Erics house I was met at the door by his mum who kindly invited me in and explained that unfortunately Eric had a really bad cold and would not be able to go out. This was in the days before mobile phones and social media.

I went through to his living room and was met by my intended in leopard design pyjamas and nearly called off the engagement there and then. My mother in law to be invited me to stay for a plate of mince and tatties which was lovely, after which they escorted me to the bus stop. I really did not want to be escorted to the bus stop as I did not think I had any money on me and was preparing to walk home. So they kindly waited with me until the bus came and they saw me safely on the bus. However as I waved them goodbye and gritted my teeth and dug in my pocket for any change, I found fifteen pence and then smiled sweetly at the driver as I asked for a ticket for as far as my fifteen pence would get me. Oh dear hen that will just get you half way along the standing stane road which is pitch black with no real pavement. I tell you what I'll drop ye off at the Gallatown if no inspector comes on board and if he does be prepared to get off immediately.

I thanked the driver and at the agreed spot alighted and walked the approximately two miles to the nurse's home. I was shattered as my footwear was not exactly best walking shoes. Anyway I shoved the kettle on and breathed a sigh of relief and sat in my chair to relax when would you believe it the blinking fire alarm went off at the hospital and I had to dash up to offer my services at the hospital. Just my luck the fire was in the tower block on the fifteenth floor and we had to evacuate the patients. By the time I had climbed all the stairs I was nearly needing oxygen myself. However I was directed to secure the fire blankets around the elderly patients in bed and start dragging the mattresses with them on top once secured to the fire exit

 I was preceded by two other student nurses who like me were nearly bursting with energy and increased adrenaline. When I followed them I heard the strangled whimper of an elderly lady who was choking on the fire blanket they had secured in their haste round her neck, poor woman nearly died of strangulation.

The poor wee soul was uncomplaining as she meekly gasped and pointed to the restraint across her neck. Her eyes emplored me to quickly release the unintended noose.

Chapter 9

Theatres and Rumbles

I was then assigned this time round to the surgical theatres and was amazed at the warren of rooms within the area. The nursing officer in charge of theatres was an eccentric older lady who was tall, imposing and a bit of tyrant whom all the staff were afraid of. We used to joke about her and particularly her appropriate name Rumbles as she constantly rumbled about most things. Her bellow of a voice reverberated throughout the theatre suite causing fear in all in hearing range.

My friend Margaret mused that what if her name was really Miss nice but to build her reputation and fear factor she decided by deed poll to change it to Rumbles.

Theatre was run on a very hierarchical system with segregation being the order of the day with the charge nurses sitting seperately from staff nurses and enrolled nurses separated from us lovely students for who knows what manner of evils may abound with familiarity.

Then when the theatres were quiet and the lists for the day were finished we lowly students were given important tasks such as folding plastic bags, cutting swabs and then folding them and if that was not enough to make us want a career in theatres we constantly cleaned all the equipment drawers. It was tedious mind numbing work that we all disliked intensely.

Still I felt more sorry for the theatre orderlies who when they had finished scrubbing theatres from top to bottom, no easy task, would groan in despair as Miss rumbles came past and told them it was not cleaned to her satisfaction and do it again.

When I think of the politically correct world we live in now and compare it with the anything goes in the time that I trained in, it was quite different.

Especially if you were an eccentric boss in the nineteen seventies it was like night and day from work environments today. It was accepted custom and practice then that eccentrics and larger than life characters were part and parcel of work life. You were expected to just get on with doing the best you can while not upsetting the status quo.

When each of the student nurses were interviewed by Miss Rumbles she engaged in what to her must have seemed chit chat but to the recipient it was an intrusive interrogation. This left them bewildered and feeling as if they had been a guest of MI5.

If the student happened to be Irish then Miss Rumbles would peer over her spectacles and ask them if any of their family were involved in the IRA proceedings in Ireland or mainland Britain. Or if in the case of Perry our Rhodesian colleague she was asked if any of her relatives were involved in the guerrilla warfare in Rhodesia.

It would be interesting to imagine how she would have responded if the Irish girls had answered in the affirmative. Yes its true Miss Rumbles my daddy and Uncle Seamus are leading members of the IRA in County Derry and have knee- capped too many folk to mention, but don't be saying anything to anyone as we don't want any bother.

As you can imagine it was not an entirely happy crew of campers who resided in the theatres and it was no surprise when bickering went on although I was surprised when I came upon two of the orderlies actually fighting. It was a short lived altercation but word got back to the oberfurher and they were called in for a wee chat and afterwards so was I.

Miss Rumbles quizzed me about what I saw and commanded me to tell all and when I insisted that really I had nothing to tell her. As in my mind I was afraid for the men's jobs and was not going to let on about it to her. When she realised that she had nothing more to gain from the conversation with me, she gave me what I can only describe as a half grin and half smirk and dismissed me.

I really enjoyed my time in theatre and found the observation of the operations intriguingly interesting seeing anatomy in the raw as opposed to the dry textbooks. When it came time for me to scrub up and head the minor procedures list I was comfortable with scrubbing up and draping and handling the small range of instruments required but that was most certainly not true of the junior doctor who was given the minor list to do on his own with me.

He was a giant of a man with size eight gloves and huge feet that barely got into his borrowed clogs. As he stumbled into theatre in his blues he enquired sheepishly what do I do for scrubbing and gowning? So began lesson one and it progressed through each stage of the list, where do I swab, where do I cut, what instrument do I use next . Well between the anaesthetist and myself and my supervisor we got him safely through the list.

It was just as well the patients were oblivious as they would have been rightly worried with this raw apprentice and it was the first time I realised that these poor doctors are often thrown in at the deep end much more so than us nurses.

One day in theatres it was a long list and my friend Margaret and I were runners and swab nurses who we were becoming more accustomed to actually understanding what was being asked for when requests were being barked at us and also finding the items requested in the storeroom.

It was a day of restrained giggles as we tried to behave ourselves in the long spells of inactivity when an amazing occurrence happened; the theatre space was immersed in this brilliant sunshine which just arrived suddenly and lit up the room in a powerful radiance.

As a Christian I was familiar with the idea that the return of Jesus would be in a flash and when least expected and so leaned over to Margaret and told her that this is what must be happening. Margaret burst out laughing and since I was not raptured into the clouds with Jesus I realised I was mistaken and we had to leave the room as we were both unable to stop giggling.

Time in theatres culminated with our end of placement report which was delivered by Miss Rumbles in her office and was not something to be anticipated. Margaret was first in to the lions den and did not come out well, when she returned to us she was in floods of tears. I took time to console her much to the consternation of the other nurses, as Miss Rumbles was in a strop and demanding the next student be sent down.

It was only when the nurses explained that Miss Rumbles would take her temper out on them if I did not hurry that I excused myself to Margaret and went into her office. I knocked and went in to see Miss Rumbles looking down at the report in front of her. After growling at me to sit down she proceeded to read from the prepared report in front of her, by this time I was quite annoyed with her for her lack of manners and upsetting my friend.

I gently interrupted her mid flow to let her I was not pleased to be given a report from someone who barely knows me and that her basic manners were quite poor. After I had finished my wee tirade she looked me up and down and said,you are the nurse I spoke with about those orderlies fighting aren't you?! I affirmed I was and it was then she smiled widely and told me I like you, when you are finished your training I will keep a job for you, to which I replied tongue in cheek I wouldn't work for you for all the tea in China you're a crabbit woman, she just laughed and told me if I ever changed my mind to call her. I never did. The other nurses were flabbergasted when I told them and could not believe my bravado, neither could I but it was heartfelt.

We came across some very interesting cases in theatres and some which made us smile such as the elderly gentleman who was admitted to the ward following a home visit by the urologist as he had acute retention of urine which was giving him a great deal of discomfort.

The consultant found to his surprise that Mr Welsh had a growth on his thigh that stretched from his groin to his knee and had been growing for a few years. During the time of the tumors growth Mr Welsh just kept asking his tailor to make new trousers for him to accommodate this change in his body shape. He did this for years rather than go and discuss this with a doctor as he had a major mistrust of them.

When he came into theatre the surgeon excavated a tumor that entirely filled a basin and weighed eight pounds, the size of a newborn baby. Thankfully the tumor turned out to be benign and he made a full recovery and no longer was troubled with retention of urine. However he would need new trousers as his odd shaped older ones were no longer needed.

One of the most shocking cases I came across in theatres was the young man who had tried to take his own life by slitting his throat and the damage was being repaired in theatre. Looking back it probably was not the most sensitive thing to do when the staff nurses called for us to go in and look at this young man of twenty three who had been unsuccessful in trying to end his own life. As the end result was shocking in its extreme. We tried to be as surreptitious as possible and try and make the acquaintance with this man as normal as possible.

Given the circumstances it was impossible to do so. So when we looked down on the result of his own hands it was like looking at a cadaver who was being worked on by medical students and left lying as they went for a tea break. His throat was slit from ear to ear and unbelievably he had missed his major arteries and his trachea otherwise he was almost decapitated.

However the most awful part was the look of hatred on his face as we spoke with him, although he never spoke a word the content of his face read with the force of the unspoken word.

He was conveying to us very clearly that he was disgusted at us interfering busybodies trying to stop him from ending his own life and that it would only be a matter of time before he made sure of doing the job properly the next time.

I felt desperately sad for this young man who was deadly serious about his mission and never did find out what had reduced him to this incredibly sad state. However I was sure he would be dead very soon after discharge from hospital.

Chapter Ten

Auxillaries and on the receiving end;

Now one breed of nurse I found who were in a league of their own was the auxillary nurse and they were formidable. Indeed in many wards they actually ran the ward according to them. In their considered opinion the only difference between them and trained nurses is the fact that they are not allowed to give out medication.

A number of them were Mrs Malaprop personified and it was particularly difficult not to laugh out loud in the light of said malapropisms. One of the best came from Joyce a tall stocky lady in her late fifties . I've just been on a posh holiday to Spain ye ken, Joyce informed me. That's nice Joyce but what made it a posh holiday, it wis because we were in a posh hotel in suet. Sorry Joyce what is in suet?

 Well obviously you've no been on a posh holiday its where you have a bathroom attached to your bedroom, oh you mean en-suite? No silly girl its in suet, you canny even say it right, oh sorry Joyce as you say I'm obviously not posh.

However one particular auxillary I owed a great deal to was Maisie in the childrens ward as she was an absolute gem and knew the workings of the ward inside out and much better than me as a new staff nurse.

The childrens ward was a very busy 30 bed general ward with surgical, medical and orthopaedic cases. It was open for emergency intakes 24 hours a day. When you are a student nurse you think you have learned a considerable amount of information but as a staff nurse you realise that your learning is just beginning. I have felt like that all my working life as I am always assimilating new information.

You were very quickly put in charge of the ward and of all the other staff despite being a very new staff nurse. It could be terrifying as each emergency admission was phoned in and we had to prepare for their arrival.

The thought of a baby or child being dependent on my knowledge and skills made my heart race but thanks to Maisie I was often very well prepared. Typically she would say, I hope you don't mind but I have laid out all the medications and equipment you may need for the acute asthmatic child we are waiting on.

Oh my word! I could have just hugged her she was an absolute star and so underrated. I found her to be more knowledgeable than many of us trained staff and such a help. I never found her to usurp any ones authority as she diligently worked away in an effort to assist us green staff nurses. I will never forget her kindness, help and support.

Eric and I had now been going out for nearly nine months and he seemed to be quite keen on me and I did really like him but as for love. Well to paraphrase the pathetic reply Prince Charles gave when asked if he was very much in love with Lady Diana, when they were announcing their engagement, well whatever love means.

That was just it I did not know if I loved Eric and if I would see us together in the long term, I could not put my finger on it and just felt I would let him go gently. I told him I saw no future for us and got on with my training.

It was at that time when I was in the middle of doing research into breast self examination regarding whether nurses and doctors practiced what they preached about self examination that I found a lump in my breast.

I was booked into the ward I had been working in for a lumpectomy as the surgeon thought it may be a fatty lump but I had to sign for a mastectomy if the biopsy carried out in theatre was found to be cancerous. I went into the ward and was put in a bay with three other women who were like me were either in for a lumpectomy or a mastectomy. They were lovely women all middle aged and like me quite nervous about the following day, I did not let them know I was a nurse until the charge nurse came to see me and greeted me as nurse McQueen and after that I was at their beck and call.

I am pleased to say that my lump was indeed a fatty lump and that it had been removed and a small scar left, however the other women did not fare so well and called on me often during my stay to assist them which I was happy to do. It was good that I was a quick healer when even the ward staff called on me to help put away the pharmacy delivery, talk about cheek, still I did not mind.

Eric had found out I was in hospital and came to visit me which was very nice of him considering I had dumped him a few days previously.

To cut a long story short we decided to try again and very soon afterwards when on a picnic in Princess street gardens in Edinburgh

Eric proposed to me but since I did not like his proposal which was I was thinking I would like it if we got engaged, I told him I would think about it. Later in the evening when I asked him if he thought I would suit diamonds?, he looked puzzled until I explained that yes I accepted his proposal and would like a diamond solitaire. Though in all honesty I thought his proposal was pants. We may have married two months before Prince Charles and Lady Diana but our marriage has lasted a lot longer. It will be our ruby wedding next year.

I did love going through to East Wemyss the wee mining village he lived in as it was so picturesque and had been used as a backdrop village for the movie Chariots of Fire.

I really took to his parents as well and particularly his dad who could not have been more different from mine if he tried. Eric's dad John was a tall quiet but an engaging gentleman, who was a Christian and said prayers before meals, never swore and went to church. Mine was short, the life and soul of the party with his drinking pals but a crabbit, morose and melancholic often violent drunk, with his family. John was also interested in having conversations about world events and enjoying general conversation over the dinner table where my dad sat on his own in front of the telly after his spell for the day in the pub and dare anyone speak while he was watching TV. We even had to leave all cupboard doors ajar to avoid any unnecessary noise upsetting dad.

We had our engagement party in my house on my twenty first birthday and my family and friends all crowed into our council house to celebrate. All of my large family as well as Eric's and our friends were to be found in all the downstairs rooms and we have a lovely picture of most of my family, complete with my dad in his very full busy red beard all perched up the stairs.

My friend Rosalind and Jim her now fiancé came as did many other friends who were now engaged. However I nearly never made the party on time as my wee clapped out mini decided to blow a tyre. I controlled the car from slewing across the road and settled by the roadside. I scrambled in the depleted set of tools for changing a tyre and looking for where the tyre was kept eventually found them and proceeded to change my first tyre. It was a messy job and my hands were covered in oil and grease but I managed to get to the house and change while the party was in its early stages.

My wee mini was my pride and joy even though it only had second and fourth gear and was horrid when you approached lights when the lights were changing as there was a danger that you would not be able to move off without being pushed around the corner. Indeed there were many occasions when that happened but the most embarrassing time was when I carried a friend and passenger who had a bad hip and pronounced limp. As we were approaching the lights I was praying for them to stay at green when they changed to red "right all out of the car and push it up the hill and over the lights", my friend Mhairi said you've got to be joking – I told her no and to hurry before the lights changed.

Chapter 11-

Whose Learning Difficulties?

Our next placements were to the learning difficulties hospitals where traditionally the mentally handicapped as we called them were incarcerated. They were placed in 30 bed wards as I mentioned earlier in institutions which were the norm for that time.

The current trend of day and community care was a long way off, following the Community Care Act of 1990. This act forced Social work departments to provide an assessment of needs and plan of care best suited to the individual. This led to the demise of large institutions as the norm and community care and a more normal life for residents. A very good way forward I felt, in an effort to improve the life of these individuals and integrate them into the community.

It was a placement that not many of us were looking forward to as we were all to a student a wee bit afraid of these strange patients who might be violent or have fits or both. It was also the first time I would be working at the same place as my mother and I was very much looking forward to that. Although my mum was only an enrolled nurse she was very able and capable of much more and indeed this was recognised in part by the hospital as she was assigned in charge of four wards on night duty and was very much respected by the nursing staff and management. I do believe had all things been equal and she had been able to undertake her registration she would have made an excellent matron.

Kay and I were sent to the low grade as they were classified then and what we now call just severe learning difficulties. In plain English they had a lot of needs and were very dependant for most of their care on us nurses. I was assigned to the low grade ward which had twenty five very dependant men in the ward and only four nurses and I was one of the four. To me it felt like I was in bedlam that Victorian madhouse where the public came to see the lunatics as they were known then.

Patients were screaming and others having fits while some of the men kept throwing their clothes off and sat about masturbating all day. I recall one man of about mid twenties who had a face only a mother could love as they say it looked like it had been ironed in and he was one of the men who stripped off his clothes all day and sat about masturbating.

One day when the window cleaners were busy at work the trained nurses asked me to take Bill for a walk around the unit. Well I was mortified because although I had seen male genitalia by this time and had bathed men, I had not had to walk a naked man anywhere and especially one with the biggest willy I had ever seen which was constantly erect and being attended to by its owner. However being junior and overruled by the senior nurses I had to oblige and was never so embarrassed in my life.

Another of the patients had cri de chat syndrome and her cry and screech was definitely high pitched and cat like and nearly burst my eardrums.

I found the staff like those in the mental health institutions just about as institutionalised as their patients and some of them were positively lazy. One evening the staff were sitting in the living area in the ward and watching Coronation street when the young girl Tracey with the cri-de-chat kept wandering around in front of the television which annoyed them. I just distracted Tracey and gave her games to play with that she liked and then went for my tea and left her in their capable care. However when I returned from tea break Tracey was stripped naked and placed in the locked cool down room. When I asked why she was placed there I was told she was being a pest and needed to cool down I knew fine well that she was bugging them as they wanted to watch tv and were too lazy to get off their backsides and actually attend to their patients, given that is what they were paid to do.

I also insisted they give the keys for me to get Tracey out of the room and afford her some dignity by putting her clothes back on her.

The nurses could be very good with the patients but also sloppy at times with keeping their knowledge and skills up to date.

Especially when decimalisation replaced imperial calculations in medicine with the new fangled at that time decimal point. To be fair it did take everyone quite some time to change from imperial measure to decimalisation.

We had to give a patient digoxin which is a drug used to assist the heart work efficiently and should not be given if the patients pulse is less than sixty beats per minute. However the trained nurse on duty had the drug in her hand and asked me cursorily to look at the drug and sign for it as she was about to give it to the patient. I asked her to check the patients pulse and after giving me an exasperated look sighed, and took it. I felt uneasy about this nurses care I checked the drug carefully and informed her she was giving one milligram and not the prescribed one hundred micrograms, she had misplaced the decimal point and was about to give an overdose of ten times the required amount.

I am going to give this as I am the trained nurse not you and both amounts you are talking about are the same. I'm afraid she would not listen to advice and being in the student role and working in the situation I was in I did not feel empowered to challenge her further.

Indeed even today in the early naughties there are still about 40,000 drug errors every year. This is not something the NHS is complacent about and indeed they are taking steps to reduce. It would seem to be an indictment of the poor numeracy and communication skills in our country at times. Although we are all human and make mistakes due to many factors.

This is something to be cognisant of and to take great care to educate nursing and medical staff. I certainly learned a valuable lesson that day with regards to the administration of medicines and the fallibility of trained nurses whom I almost to that point thought to be infallible.

A group of people I just loved working with were those patients with Downs syndrome or Mongols as they were sometimes called in those days, but now that term is seen to be derisory. They were just the happiest people and very loving folk and always looking for a hug. If you ever felt down a day you were on duty they soon banished your woes especially as they were often wanting to dance to any music that was on at the time.

However the part I hated most at the hospital was meal times as it seemed so undignified and barbaric where we liquidised everything and believe it or not added red sauce to every meal even puddings. We then had all patients strapped into chairs with tables in front of them (Buxton chairs) and the practice we were taught was to stand at the back of the patient and tip the chair back and feed this mush into the patient from behind. It was a loathsome practice and I complained about it continually but was always overruled.

 I know I would have hated to have been fed like this. Yet the terror the patients must have felt at being subjected to this ordeal was unknown fully but clearly palpable.

What I didn't understand at the time was that was the thing about institutionalisation, the needs of the organisation came before the needs of the patient and holistic individual care was a long way off.

Chapter 12-

Nearing the end of the beginning;

Our last placement before qualifying as registered nurses was with the district nurses in the community.

Nursing in the community in Fife in the late nineteen seventies was eventful to say the least. I was assigned to the Links medical practice which had a sizeable caseload of patients from very deprived backgrounds. I recall going to do a bed bath for an elderly lady in a flat with my colleague and since we had no reply to our call for entry we entered and started the search for the old lady. The house was a total midden and utterly piled high with all sorts of ephemera. We looked in one room and it was piled high with rubbish, papers and old dirty clothes and in the corner was a dilapidated old bed piled with old rags. We turned to go and heard an almost imperceptible moan and lo and behold found our patient. Mrs Burns was wizened, emaciated and quite frankly looked like the living dead, poor wee soul. Our uniform for the community was a white dress black shoes, blue cap and Burberry coat. So when we were clambering over the piles of rubbish I was frightened rats would jump out. It made me quite sick to think a human being was reduced to existing like this in a first world country.

As I love architecture and homes I loved going to see the layout of peoples homes when we went on a community visit. I once went to a beautiful Victorian home to do a leg dressing on an elderly gentleman. His daughter who house he shared opened the door to me and I remarked how lovely her house was. She asked if I wanted to have a look around and of course I did, it was stunning. There were so many period features, nooks and crannies and antique furniture. Once the tour was over I thanked her and exclaimed again how beautiful her home was as I was heading to go out the door. Just before my hand reached the door handle she said excuse me but have you forgotten fathers dressing. Oops a wee bit embarrassing but I apologised and went up the stairs to complete the task I had actually come for.

We combined our spell on community with a short placement with the health visitor and I have to say in all honesty it taught me that the last job I wanted to do was become a health visitor. The baby clinics to me were a nightmare with all those crying babies and weepy mums. They were paranoid that their baby was not progressing as well as the woman next to her who seemingly had a wonder baby.

Then there were the characters who made up the health visiting fraternity, quite a number of them single women who had never reared a child in their life and yet theoretically they were alleged experts.

My friend Perri was a black Rhodesian lady who was landed with Miss Smythe a stocky woman in her mid fifties. She was a snob and officious lady who laid down the law to the women in her caseload. I don't think she intentionally meant to be mean but she came from the old school of thinking that Nurse knows best so best do what nurse tells you.

It was the dead of a very cold winter when we did health visiting and the snow was often thick on the ground and we had to often dig the car wheels free from the snow. At the end of a shift all of the students would congregate in the nurses home and swop stories of the days and its proceedings. Wee Perri came in chittering of the cold and we commiserated with her as the climate in Rhodesia (now Zimbabwe) we realised must have been very different from ours. Perri explained that Miss Smythe would not let her go into the houses with her as it was confidential information and made her sit in the car for over an hour at a time. We were never sure if she was racist as well as officious but it gave Perri a very bad cold and did nothing to warm any of us to that lady or health visiting in general.

We all studied very hard to be able to pass our final exams and become a registered general nurse.

It was partly due to my nurse training and encountering all the people I had the honour and privilege of nursing that made me want to find out a bit more about my complex father.

I sat with mum one evening when dad was at the pub when she told me some of the background to the complexities of his character.

Dad was the oldest of four children to our gran and Dai (granddad). Gran was not the cuddly type and quite frightening to us as children. We would go and visit her and Dai who would be sitting watching television and would happily chat with us. He would slip us a sixpence (2.5 pence in todays money but worth a lot to us as children then) and tell us not to tell gran. When we were on our way out of the door we would say goodbye to Dai and gran would let us out of the door. Her hand would be extended palm upwards and she would snarl, give me the sixpence your Dai gave you, we are pensioners you know. We would meekly hand back the sixpence and go home to mum, if gran was in a good mood she would exchange the sixpence for a halfpenny.

Gran was a narcissist according to those I spoke with and seemed to think life had not given her fair share of whatever she thought she deserved. So she took it out on others, certainly my dad had his share of her mean and moody behaviour. It was rumoured that Gran had an affair in the war with a polish soldier and the result was our uncle Alfie. Certainly he was a favoured son whom she fed better than others and showed more love to him, than my dad received.

Both my dad and Alfie were miners, a hard demanding and physical job. So when they came home from the pits they looked forward to their meal at night. One time both men sat down to their food, Alfie had his plate piled high with stew and mash potatoes and my dad got a boiled egg as gran said that's all that was left.

Needless to say dad escaped from the house as soon as he could, aged 19 years and joined the army as a gunner in the royal artillery regiment of Scotland.

He served as a member of the United Nations forces in the Korean War in 1950-1953. He joined up with his best pal Archie and soon they found themselves in heavy fighting at the Mancurian line. During a lull in the fighting the two other men, his pal Archie and their friend John were taking a smoke break. Dad recalls chatting with Archie about what they will do when the war is over and he was rolling a cigarette. His head was down concentrating on the cigarette when he remembers a loud bang. The firing had recommenced and their area was hit. When he regained consciousness he found his pal John had the heavy barrel of the 25 pounder artillery gun lying over his legs and was squirming in agony. He amazingly lifted to weight from off Johns legs to free him. He then looked for Archie, to discover he had taken the brunt of the explosion and was literally in pieces. Dad collected Archies body parts and bagged them so he could be buried with honour. Once dad had completed these awful tasks, he fell into the mud unconscious as he had severe burns over his face, neck, arms and chest. Fortunately for dad he was retrieved quickly by the medical team and sent to the hospital in Soeul for treatment.

They were astounded at how well he healed as the churned up wet mud they were fighting in had in effect protected his skin. All his life he had problems with his wrists which may have been a consequence of lifting the heavy gun barrel from Johns legs. John survived the ordeal also and owed his life to dads strength and presence of mind. Dad was mentioned in despatches and awarded a medal which was sent to his home and his lovely mother binned it.

What an experience for a young man, firstly he was poorly nurtured with a cold and narcissistic mother and then had the horrific experience in the field of war. In those days post traumatic stress disorder was not a recognised condition and soldiers were expected to just get on with life.

So although I cannot condone my dads behaviour I can certainly understand some of the reason for it.

So the big day came and we all sat our final exams and all bar one of us passed and we were now able to call ourselves a Registered General Nurse. Such joy at our achievements but a wee bit sadness at the thought that we were all splitting up to go our separate ways as we looked for our first posts as Staff Nurses. Although as it is said it was not the end only the beginning of a long, varied and very interesting career that to me at that time was yet unknown.

I opted to apply for midwifery training and was accepted onto the course in 1980. I had many interesting times and experiences during that eventful year.

Chapter 13 – (or 12a for the Superstitious)

Onto Midwifery

Well two months following my qualifying as a staff nurse I embarked on my midwifery training. This was done over the period of a year as we were already qualified as general nurses and were accredited with prior learning.

We still had to achieve certain milestones and skills such as 40 deliveries within the year, so many episiotomies and so on and so forth. Today most midwives are direct entry and so you can enter as a 17 year old and be qualified before the age of 21. My personal view is that it is better to have life experience first as well as general training as it's the foundation to all care. However a friend of mine Claire did direct entry many years ago and has thrived on it despite my recommendations to do general first.

Our college was world renowned for midwifery training and we had students from the UK, Ireland, Australia and Rhodesia amongst other places. We were signed into achieving at least a 60% pass rate in all exams as the standards were high to maintain good quality student midwives. Indeed when our marks were dipping near 60% we were counselled and basically expected to put in greater effort. We were actually expected to achieve 75% and more and very many of us did. It seemed harsh at first and especially given the tutors were exceedingly pernickety. If we were given a definition of for example a justo minor pelvis, (this is a pelvis which has reduced internal diameters of up to 1cm, not much but difficult for baby to get through) and did not put in every word of their definition we were marked as a fail and nil point given. Two of our colleagues Joan and Mhairi, the old women in the class, who were possibly just in their late thirties had to be counselled and moved back a year as they hovered between 50-60% pass rates. Joan went on to have a very successful career, becoming a charge midwife and being awarded an MBE for services to midwifery. She is a good friend and excellent alternative medicine practitioner.

We had about 40 students in the class, all women and mostly about my age early twenties. We had about a dozen southern Irish girls who spoke so fast and with such a broad accent that it took us a bit of time to tune in and understand them. They were not amused initially at having to repeat themselves but we did laugh when we followed them into the wards as they spoke with the women.

We would hang back at the door to witness the spectacle as it was always funny. The expectant mothers looked and felt just as we had, it was a mixture of embarrassment and fear at offending them. When we first heard them, even though they were speaking English, their accent made them sound like distinctly foreign.

When they went into the wards to work they would step forward and say Good Morning Mrs Smith I am Breda and I am a new midwifery student, so I will be looking after you today.

Now we knew that's what they were saying as we were now attuned to their twang, however the women would just hear blurh blurgh blurgh for a couple of minutes. Their faces were a picture, here they were often first time mums to be and awaiting induction for labour, something of a worry to them.

So to be faced with a student midwife who would be looking after them and speaking rapidly in what sounded like a foreign language, was a worry to them.

. The girls spoke so quickly in what could have been Gaelic, Mexican or Spanish that the expectant mums could not make head nor tale of what was being said to them.

We surmised that the next thoughts in the stricken minds of the mums to be would be, Oh my goodness, here and I about to commence labour and these smiling women who speak no English are looking after me. I am going to die and my baby will be orphaned and I will never see them, how will I cope, how will my husband cope?

At least that's what we deducted from their terror stricken faces as we would silently laugh at the situation before offering ourselves as interpretors.

In time the Irish girls toned down their accent and our ears attuned to their dialect, as did those of the expectant mothers. I thought Fifers spoke quickly but the Irish girls were in a league of their own, they went off like racehorses at the Grand National race, who had gone off before the starter gun sounded.

Also at the end of every sentence they would add God bless them, what a laugh they were, we enjoyed their company.

Our tutors seemed positively posh, dignified and incredibly knowledgeable compared to our general training tutors. They were dare I say it a wee bit prim and proper, stiff upper lip and all that jazz. Though they were approachable and very keen that we did well and were able to maintain the 100% pass rate at the college. Unbeknown to outsiders that's because those not achieving were counselled out or moved down a year. However the rest of us motley crew were determined to do well and become the best midwives we could be.

Once again in my training I met some crackers of midwives and tutors, eccentrics of the highest order to my mind. At the old maternity hospital I was introduced to Sister Francis our clinical tutor. Myself and Julie were assigned together and Miss Frances introduced herself to us and announced today I will show you around and then go over a delivery of a baby again with you. So far so good until she decided I must have looked about 9 years of age and needed to take my hand while showing us around the maternity unit.
It was quite a strange experience, firstly having your hand held by your tutor and being told the obvious such as and this is the telephone. There was certainly a few interesting characters when I was training.

I started off my learning in the delivery suite with the irrepressible and slightly bonkers Sister Gilchrist. She was tall and slim with short dark hair and was known to be a bit a stickler for her rules however eccentric the rules seemed. I was to learn more of them as each shift passed.

I had learned the theory of how to deliver a baby of course but here I was in the real deal and gearing my mind and spirit up, to deliver the precious cargo safely to the mums I encountered.

As usual I was all excited about new experiences and new firsts and of course I had a quota of 40 babies to deliver within my years training. I would wait eagerly and pop in often to the labouring mothers rooms and check on their progress and be prepared to gown up in preparation for my first delivery. It was both exciting and terrifying as I didn't want to mess up so possibly went into the rooms more often than was expected.

I heard a women groan and call for help as she said she thought she needed to push.

I was just about to go into the room to check and see if the babies head was visible when I heard Sister Gilchrist shout down at me what do you think you are doing ? I replied that Mrs Smith said she needed to push and I was going to check. Come away from that room girl she said , I can tell from here whether or not she needs to push and she is not ready.

Well as she brooked no argument and I was a greenhorn and her junior by a long way I had to pull back. How strange I thought this was most certainly not in the training I had received thus far.

However five minutes later Mrs Smith screamed help me and I went in to find the babies head almost delivered, I popped my head out the door and called for help. I then went back in the room and only had time to get one glove on never mind the full regalia of gown and gloves. Then in a few minutes baby john was born, my first delivery, phew mother and baby alive and well and a wee bit shocked me pleased at the outcome, I think.

My first five deliveries were all more or less like this one due to Sister Gilchrists odd rules. I thought she was bonkers but got to know her quite well as she took a shine to me. I discovered later that if she liked you she would help you in any way she could but if she didn't well woe betide you?

I did come to see that although she seemed impatient with the parous women, that's women who have had babies before. She had infinite patience for the single women and those were primigravid, that is first time mums. It was like watching a female version of Jeckyl and Hyde at work in some ways as her character was quite at odds with itself.

In my year training I delivered over 55 babies and only had a couple of really scary moments, such as when I thought I had broken the babys neck. The babys mother was diabetic and although not obese was a stocky lady and short in stature, her baby was thought to be a big baby and true to form the baby was a fair size and it became stuck at the shoulders, though not a true shoulder dystocia.

Now Sister Kenny had been a medical missionary in Africa and was used to most things and could think of solutions others couldn't. I was so glad to have her as my supervisor that day. The way to free the shoulders was to place both hands on either side of the babies head and pull down hard when mother is pushing with a contraction. I was fairly strong and was pulling with all my might to no avail. Sister advised to drop the lower half of the bed to allow me more traction. Again I pulled and pulled when all of a sudden I felt a give and I heard a terrible grating, crunching sound from where my hands were. I was both terrified and mortified and whispered to sister to check baby as I thought I had broken babys neck. Thankfully it was a wee tissue tear of mothers perineum and not babys neck. I then breathed out and safely delivered baby to his delighted mum.

The mothers placenta failed to deliver and Sister Kenny employed a technique she had used often in Africa to manually remove the placenta in the delivery room to spare the mum an anaesthetic and theatre.

Years later when I was working back in the maternity hospital I heard the recall of a very experienced obstetrician who in his last year of work had taken a sabbatical to work three months in Ghana. He told us many interesting stories about how he delivered so many babies and used so many techniques he had never deployed in Scotland. This was so women did not need to have surgery and needed to be quickly mobile to return to their villages. He said that he felt that all obstetricians would do well to do an occasional stint in an African or third world country to learn how to deal with difficult deliveries. He felt he had learned more in three months than he had in the last twenty years in the UK.

I recall a story one of our missionaries from the church we attended told us about childbirth and its dangers and the logical but unusual solutions used in Botswana.

Margaret was a senior midwife and tutor in charge of a maternity hospital in Botswana and was informed of a lady and her two friends coming to the hospital. The women had walked 3 days to get help. The lady was in labour in the village 3 days ago but all contractions had stopped. Mother was exhausted and feeling unwell, only with the help and encouragement of her friends did she somehow manage to find the strength and determination to walk for three days.

Margaret examined the lady and for the life of her could not determine what way the baby was lying inside the mother. The mother was almost incoherent with a fever and so exhausted that Margaret took more clinical history from the two friends.

What transpired was both shocking and astonishing but at the end of the day quite logical in its conclusion. The mother had a long labour and the baby seemed to be progressing slowly but surely down the birth canal. However with the Dula in attendance, a villager who though untrained had delivered many babies, had tried to assist with the delivery. The baby's head had delivered as normal but it had then become stuck and the Dula could not get the baby out, however much she tried. The ladies of the village knew they had to get help but that without transport the nearest hospital was the mission led one which was three days away. If they did not get help the mother of two other children may die. A solution was needed and the best one they could think of to allow the mother to walk with them was to cut the baby's head off. This may seem barbaric to you and I but it was a solution and it did indeed save the mothers life as she had a caesarean section and recovered in a clean and well equipped hospital.

I am full of admiration for these strong, resolute and hardy women who did the best they could in the worst of circumstances.

It is a known fact that if you have an extremley rare complication of twins, they occur 1 in 90,000 times. If the babies heads become locked when being delivered vaginally, to save one of them it may be necessary to decapitate the other twin to allow safe progress, if the delivery is advanced and all else has failed.

If it is known the heads are locked early enough they can be delivered by caesarean section. So the women in Africa were taking a stoical needs must approach.

After the delivery suite I moved onto the postnatal ward which was a long Nightingale ward with 12 beds only divided by curtains for privacy if required. In the middle of the room was a long pine table for the women to have their breakfast in the morning.

Now this may sound like a good idea all mothers together providing care and support to each other as they gaily toiled away learning how to be a mother. In my day mothers stayed in hospital for about 7 days and today a mother may be discharged within 6 hours of giving birth.

However the maternal Nightingale ward to me seemed like a nightmare that was not easily escaped. You had crying babies all the time, then you had competitive mothers boasting how big and healthy their baby was, but never mind dear your wee tiny boy will grow big and strong like mine one day.

Throw some hormones into the mix and you have hormonal and tired mothers who had barely slept becoming more insecure and wearied with each passing day. Only the robust and previously travelled survived this trial by torture.

If you then add insult to injury I worked with a staff nurse who would have been in her mid to late 50's at the time but to my youth seemed ancient. I wasn't sure if her motorised scooter was parked nearby for a quick escape at home time. This nurse at first accounts seemed friendly, calm and sweet until she noted something that troubled her.

Oh my word I was shocked when it happened, the ladies were all sat at the breakfast table chattering away amicably, babies all peaceful thankfully. Then without a word of a lie this nurse came striding into the room and slammed her hand down on the table which the sound alone shocked the women to fright and silence.

Then she said in her best hissing voice that was laced with menace and disgust, your babies have all lost weight today and I am not happy about this. She then strode manfully out of the room after delivering the news. Leaving me alone with all the women.

Well at this point without exception all the mums burst into tears and started to ask between tears and the sniffles and snot of distressed, hormonal and sleep deprived women. What is wrong with my baby? Have I done something wrong? I calmed the ladies down eventually and went to find out the weights of the babies. They were all within the allowable 10% weight loss expected of babies less than 10 days old.

I look back on that incident and consider why that seemingly kindly docile nurse acted so out of character and slipped into Atilla the Hun's shoes for a nanosecond. My conclusion the menace of hormones in a menopausal woman, otherwise I was working with another Jeckyl and Hyde character.

Well I encountered so many characters in my career that my book would be boring without them, so to every one of you I met and worked with, thankyou.

On our community placement within our midwifery training it was an eye opener visiting folks in their own homes. It was the dead of a very cold winter it wasn't particularly pleasant for us to work in our less than practical dress uniforms. To add insult to injury I did a joint visit with the midwife in a home that stank of body odour, and extremely poor hygiene. I was asked to nip upstairs to do a quick check on the new mother while the midwife would check baby over downstairs. I took off my Burberry coat and gingerly draped it over the arm of the sofa. I went upstairs and into the bedroom I was directed to where the new mother and father were still reclined in bed. I indicated who I was and the need to check the mother. I had to ask the father to move over the bed to allow me to assess the mother, he was none to pleased, they seemed put out at our visit. I quickly did what was required and went downstairs to collect my coat and get out of the stinking house. I was struck by the amazing collection of brass plaques displayed on the wall which were immaculate and highly polished. As I put my coat on my nostrils stung with the smell and I hurried outside. My coat now stunk to high heaven, so much so that I refused to wear it the rest of the day in case the patients thought it was me who stunk. I was frozen by the end of the shift. I never could understand why some people and especially if you are young or able do not keep themselves and their home clean. If only they took as much pride in cleaning themselves as much as they did their brasses.

Following the community placement stint we went back to college for further training. It was during class one day we heard snippets of news being released that the nurses home in the hospital had been on fire in the early hours of the morning and that at least one of the nurses had died. As many of us had friends still in the nurses home we could not settle so we were allowed to phone and find out the situation.

It transpired that the home a five storey building had been on fire, caused by an electrical fault sparking and then travelling quickly along the floors by the polystyrene tiles on the ceilings. This caused lots of smoke and fumes and much panic. One of the nurses realised the building was on fire and called the fire brigade. It was in the early hours of the morning when all the nurses were asleep in their beds. By the time the alarm was raised the fire had taken hold and was quickly traversing the corridors. Most of the nurses were barricaded in their rooms as the flames consumed the flammables and danced at the doors with a destructive force, looking for more to assuage its hunger.

The senior night nurse had been informed and prior to the arrival of the fire brigade and had entered the building with a female police officer to alert the nurses and get them out. They crawled low due to the thick billowing smoke and got as far as the third floor when they had to go back for their own safety as the smoke was so dense.

The fire service were on the scene within minutes but had come to the roadside and many of the nurses higher up were situated on the opposite side of the building. The RAF were also called to assist any nurses who may have climbed on the roof. Ten nurses were taken to safety via the fire service hydrolic platform.

The nurses on the opposite side of the building were terrified and desperately afraid for their lives so a number of them threw out their mattresses onto the concrete below and started to jump out. A porter caught one of the nurses and helped break the fall of another but in total 17 nurses were badly injured.

One nurse who had jumped and had severe injuries and needed treatment in Edinburgh recalled the night, once she had recovered and was back home. She said she awoke coughing and spluttering as the smoke sneaked into her room. She heard more noise and confusion and gingerly opened the door to be met by more smoke and flames. She put some material at the door to try and block out the smoke and went to the window to shout for help. The rescuers told her to stay still as they would get to her, she waited for what seemed like an eternity. Then when she saw the flames starting to consume her door she realised that she didn't want to be burned to death and thought the only escape was to jump.

She told my friend that just before she jumped she thought I'm not leaving behind my nice new underwear I bought from Marks and Spencer that day and so with her new pants in her hand she jumped out in her nightdress. Remarkably she laughed when she recounted, here I was jumping to save my life, new knickers in hand and none on under my nightie as it flew up in the air.

Very sadly when the fire was under control a young nurse was discovered dead, lying in the corridor where she had been overcome with fumes.

It was never used again as a nurses home and is now an administration block. The nursing officer was awarded an MBE for her bravery and many others were commended for their bravery that terrible night of terror.

Our maternity hospital in Kirkcaldy had a cottage hospital feel to it and everyone knew everyone else. It was mostly good to work and learn in and I was honoured to have a number of babies named after me. I do recall one couple whose baby I delivered who although delighted with the safe arrival were sad that it was not a girl as they wanted to name the baby after me. I was just pleased for them that all was well with their new family. A few minutes later the dad came running after me and said we have decided to give our son the middle name Lorne which is in thanks to you, so sweet.

The first time I did night duty at the hospital as a student midwife I was in the post natal ward. I was in charge of the ward as the other trained member of staff was a staff nurse and not a midwife. However she was a very capable nurse with many years experience and most likely knew a considerable amount more me.
I am sure by the end of the shift the nurse thought I was just a hindrance. This was due to me spending most of the night in the toilet, as I had an upset stomach, due I think to my body being shocked about working overnight for the first time.

We absolutely loved our meal times in the maternity hospital at night time as we had a cook who cooked us fresh meals overnight. The cook would call each ward and ask us if we wanted food and then would offer us a for example a choice of scampi or mince and potatoes. Changed days now as there are vending machines with sandwiches and sweets for night staff.

Our final exams were both practical and theory, with the practical element being held in Edinburgh. True to form we all passed with flying colours and were now able to call ourselves midwives.
We all applied for jobs but unfortunately there were few to be had and I was offered a job with the elderly which I declined.

I therefore applied for and accepted a post as a staff nurse in the paediatric ward and never did return to midwifery. So a new chapter of my life began and many new experiences which have been exciting, scary and humbling.
Do join me to discover more of these adventures and the characters I was to meet and share in their lives in my next book.

About the Author

Lorna is an Advanced Neonatal Nurse Practitioner and is still working in a Neonatal unit as she lives and works in the Kingdom of Fife.

Lorna has been married to Eric for almost 40 years and has three adult children and 4 adorable grandchildren.

Lorna has worked in education, business and nursing throughout her working life.

She is also an Aesthetics practitioner and a Celebrant.

In her spare time she enjoys reading and writing as well as walking cycling and travelling.

Lorna would be delighted to hear from you reader regarding what you think of her book and if you would be interested to read more in this genre. Contact her at lornafinlay@icloud.com

She is currently writing two follow up books which will be full of the characters and truly amazing patients she was privileged to meet in nursing, teaching and in business.

Printed in Poland
by Amazon Fulfillment
Poland Sp. z o.o., Wrocław

59501419R00092